EDITOR: Maryanne Blacker
FOOD EDITOR: Pamela Clark

• • •

ART DIRECTOR: Paula Wooller
DESIGNER: Robbylee Phelan

• • •

DEPUTY FOOD EDITOR: Jan Castorina
ASSISTANT FOOD EDITOR: Kathy Snowball
ASSOCIATE FOOD EDITOR: Enid Morrison
SENIOR HOME ECONOMISTS: Alexandra McCowan, Louise Patniotis, Kathy Wharton
HOME ECONOMISTS: Cynthia Black, Leisel Chen, Bronwen Clark, Kathy McGarry, Tracey Port, Maggie Quickenden, Dimitra Stais
EDITORIAL COORDINATOR: Elizabeth Hooper
KITCHEN ASSISTANT: Amy Wong

• • •

STYLISTS: Marie-Helene Clauzon, Carolyn Fienberg, Jane Hann, Jacqui Hing, Rosemary de Santis
PHOTOGRAPHERS: Kevin Brown, Robert Clark, Robert Taylor, Jon Waddy

• • •

HOME LIBRARY STAFF

ASSISTANT EDITOR: Beverley Hudec
EDITORIAL COORDINATOR: Fiona Nicholas

• • •

ACP PUBLISHER: Richard Walsh
ACP DEPUTY PUBLISHER: Nick Chan

• • •

Produced by The Australian Women's Weekly Home Library.
Typeset by ACP Colour Graphics Pty Ltd. Printed by Dai Nippon Co., Ltd in Japan.
Published by ACP Publishing Pty Ltd, 54 Park Street, Sydney.
♦ AUSTRALIA: Distributed by Network Distribution Company, 54 Park Street Sydney, (02) 282 8777.
♦ UNITED KINGDOM: Distributed in the U.K. by Australian Consolidated Press (UK) Ltd, 20 Galowhill Rd, Brackmills, Northampton NN4 OEE (0604) 760 456.
♦ CANADA: Distributed in Canada by Whitecap Books Ltd, 1086 West 3rd St, North Vancouver V7P 3J6 (604) 980 9852.
♦ NEW ZEALAND: Distributed in New Zealand by Netlink Distribution Company, 17B Hargreaves St, Level 5, College Hill, Auckland 1 (9) 302 7616.
♦ SOUTH AFRICA: Distributed in South Africa by Intermag, PO Box 57394, Springfield 2137 (011) 493 3200.

• • •

Quick-Mix Cakes

Includes index.
ISBN 1 86396 001 5.

1. Cookery. 2. Entertaining. (Series: Australian Women's Weekly Home Library).

641.5'68

• • •

• • •

COVER: Cherry Coconut Cake, page 78.
China from Villeroy & Boch; coffee pot, sugar bowl, creamer and serviette ring from Vasa Agencies; painted background from FX Designs.
OPPOSITE: Family-Sized Buttery Vanilla Cake, page 20.
BACK COVER: Apple and Custard Muffins; Fresh Blueberry Muffins, page 114.

QUICK CAKES

We used very easy mixing methods to create a magnificent array of cakes and muffins without fiddle or fuss, and next to no washing up. You simply place all ingredients into one bowl or a saucepan, mix or stir them all together, then cook. Even the children can get into the act! The key points are to weigh and measure accurately, use cake pans and select oven temperatures as specified. You can mix and match our icings, frostings and fillings with the cakes you choose, or follow the ideas in our photographs. We tested our cakes in conventional gas and electric ovens but, if in doubt, check the manufacturer's instructions.

Pamela Clark
FOOD EDITOR

BRITISH & NORTH AMERICAN READERS: Please note that Australian cup and spoon measurements are metric. A quick conversion guide appears on page 127.
A glossary explaining unfamiliar terms and ingredients appears on page 124.

One Bowl Method

Scrumptious chocolate cakes are undeniably the stars of this enormous section, but delights include fruit cakes, butter cakes, dessert-type cakes, lunch box cakes and lots of surprises – all easy with an electric mixer and just one bowl.

OUR TIPS FOR SUCCESS

■ We have used an electric mixer to make the cakes in this section. A mixer attached to a stand or a hand-held electric mixer are both suitable, but do not use a blender, food processor or hand-held processor. It is possible to beat the mixtures using a wooden spoon, but this is laborious and time-consuming, and the results will rarely be as good.

■ We have indicated when to use small, medium or large bowls; these decisions were based on accommodating the finished mixture.

■ It doesn't matter in which order the ingredients are added to the bowl, but make sure the butter is soft, but not melted, before adding other ingredients. If the butter is beginning to lose its shape or is melted, the cake will be heavy.

■ In some cases, all the ingredients are combined in the bowl, then mixed. In other cases, solid ingredients such as fruit and nuts are inappropriate to mix with the electric mixer as they could damage the beaters. They are stirred in at the end of the mixing.

■ Once you have the ingredients in the bowl, go ahead with making the cake; do not leave them standing in the bowl.

■ When mixing these mixtures, use a low speed and scrape the mixture with a rubber or plastic spatula into the path of the beaters. Once all the ingredients are mixed, gradually increase the speed to about medium and continue to beat and scrape the mixture towards the beaters until the mixture appears to be smooth and/or well mixed and slightly changed in colour. We have stated when not to over-beat. As a rule, the whole mixing time is around 3 minutes.

■ As a rule, castor sugar is used for these cakes as it gives a slightly finer texture than ordinary crystal sugar; do not attempt to dissolve the sugar during the beating process. Do not substitute honey or raw or demerara sugar for white or brown sugar; the results will be quite different.

■ Eggs and milk are best used at room temperature, but this is not essential.

QUICK-MIX PATTY CAKES

125g butter, chopped
1 teaspoon vanilla essence
¾ cup (165g) castor sugar
2 eggs
1½ cups (225g) self-raising flour
½ cup (125ml) milk

Line 2 x 12-hole deep patty pan trays with paper patty cases.

Combine all ingredients in medium bowl of electric mixer, beat on low speed until ingredients are combined. Then, beat on medium speed until mixture is smooth and changed in colour. Drop 1½ tablespoons of mixture into paper cases. Bake in moderate oven about 20 minutes. Turn onto wire rack to cool.

If desired, make cakes into butterfly or fairy cakes, fill with 1 quantity Chantilly Cream (page 121) and dust with sifted icing sugar.

RIGHT: Quick-Mix Patty Cakes.

Basket from Butler & Co.

CHOCOLATE BUTTER CAKE

185g butter, chopped
¾ cup (165g) castor sugar
3 eggs
1 cup (150g) self-raising flour
½ cup (75g) plain flour
⅓ cup (35g) cocoa
½ cup (125ml) milk

Grease deep 20cm round cake pan, cover base with baking paper.

Combine all ingredients in medium bowl of electric mixer, beat on low speed until ingredients are combined. Then, beat on medium speed until mixture is smooth and changed in colour. Pour mixture into prepared pan. Bake in moderate oven about 1 hour. Stand few minutes before turning onto wire rack to cool.

Top cold cake with 1 quantity Chocolate Fudge Frosting (page 121) and chocolate curls (page 122), if desired.

ANY TIME CHOCOLATE CAKE

125g butter, melted
1 cup (220g) castor sugar
2 eggs
1 cup (150g) self-raising flour
¼ cup (25g) cocoa
½ cup (125ml) milk

Grease 20cm ring pan, cover base with baking paper.

Combine all ingredients in small bowl of electric mixer, beat on low speed until ingredients are combined. Then, beat on medium speed until mixture is smooth and changed in colour. Pour mixture into prepared pan. Bake in moderate oven about 40 minutes. Stand few minutes before turning onto wire rack to cool.

Top cold cake with 1 quantity Chocolate Vienna Cream Frosting (page 121) and decorate with walnuts, if desired.

ABOVE: From left: Chocolate Butter Cake, Any Time Chocolate Cake.
ABOVE RIGHT: Clockwise from left: Poppy Seed Lemon Cake, Almond Caraway Cake, Caraway Seed Cake.

Above: China from Royal Doulton. Above right: Platters from Windsor Antique Market; floral fabric from Les Olivades.

POPPY SEED LEMON CAKE

185g butter, chopped
2 teaspoons grated lemon rind
1 cup (220g) castor sugar
3 eggs
2 cups (300g) self-raising flour
3/4 cup (180ml) milk
1/3 cup (55g) poppy seeds

Grease 15cm x 25cm loaf pan, cover base with baking paper.

Combine butter, rind, sugar, eggs, flour and milk in medium bowl of electric mixer, beat on low speed until ingredients are combined. Then, beat on medium speed until mixture is smooth and changed in colour. (Mixture might appear to be curdled at this stage, but will reconstitute later.) Stir in seeds. Pour mixture into prepared pan. Bake in moderate oven about 1 hour. Stand 5 minutes before turning onto wire rack to cool.

Top cold cake with 1/2 quantity Lemon Vienna Cream Frosting (page 121), if desired.

ALMOND CARAWAY CAKE

185g butter, chopped
1/2 teaspoon almond essence
2 teaspoons grated lemon rind
1 cup (220g) castor sugar
3 eggs
2 cups (300g) self-raising flour
1 tablespoon ground almonds
1/4 cup (60ml) milk
3 teaspoons caraway seeds

Grease 23cm square slab cake pan, cover base with baking paper.

Combine butter, essence, rind, sugar, eggs, flour, nuts and milk in medium bowl of electric mixer, beat on low speed until ingredients are combined. Then, beat on medium speed until mixture is smooth and changed in colour. Stir in seeds. Spread mixture into prepared pan. Bake in moderate oven about 40 minutes. Stand few minutes before turning onto wire rack to cool.

Top cold cake with 1 quantity Orange Vienna Cream Frosting (page 121), if desired.

CARAWAY SEED CAKE

125g butter, chopped
1 cup (220g) castor sugar
2 eggs
1 1/4 cups (185g) self-raising flour
1/4 cup (30g) custard powder
1/2 cup (125ml) milk
2 tablespoons caraway seeds

Grease 14cm x 21cm loaf pan, cover base with baking paper.

Combine butter, sugar, eggs, flour, custard powder and milk in medium bowl of electric mixer, beat on low speed until ingredients are combined. Then, beat on medium speed until mixture is smooth and changed in colour. Stir in seeds. Spoon and spread mixture into prepared pan. Bake in moderately slow oven about 1 hour. Stand few minutes before turning onto wire rack to cool.

Dust cold cake with sifted icing sugar, if desired.

LEMON YOGURT CAKE

125g butter, chopped
2 teaspoons grated lemon rind
1 cup (220g) castor sugar
2 eggs
1½ cups (225g) self-raising flour
¾ cup (180ml) plain yogurt
⅓ cup (55g) mixed peel

Grease 14cm x 21cm loaf pan, cover base with baking paper.

Combine butter, rind, sugar, eggs, flour and yogurt in medium bowl of electric mixer, beat on low speed until ingredients are combined. Then, beat on medium speed until mixture is smooth and changed in colour. Stir in mixed peel. Spread mixture into prepared pan. Bake in moderate oven about 1 hour. Stand few minutes before turning onto wire rack to cool.

Top cold cake with ½ quantity Vienna Cream Frosting (page 121) and extra mixed peel, if desired.

BUTTERY BUTTERSCOTCH CAKE

250g butter, chopped
1 cup (200g) firmly packed
**   brown sugar**
2 eggs
1 tablespoon golden syrup
1½ cups (225g) self-raising flour
½ cup (125ml) milk

Grease deep 20cm round cake pan, cover base with baking paper.

Combine all ingredients in medium bowl of electric mixer, beat on low speed until ingredients are combined. Then, beat on medium speed until mixture is smooth and changed in colour. Spread mixture into prepared pan. Bake in moderate oven about 50 minutes. Stand 10 minutes before turning onto wire rack to cool.

Dust cold cake with sifted icing sugar, if desired.

ABOVE: Lemon Yogurt Cake.
RIGHT: From back: Buttery Butterscotch Cake, Golden Caramel Cake.

Above: Napery from Country Road Homewear; wire tray from Horgan Imports. Right: China from Windsor Antique Market; fabric from I. Redelman & Son Pty. Ltd.

GOLDEN CARAMEL CAKE

185g butter
¾ cup (150g) firmly packed
    brown sugar
2 eggs
⅓ cup (80ml) golden syrup
1½ cups (225g) self-raising flour
½ cup (75g) plain flour
¾ cup (180ml) milk

Grease 21cm baba cake pan. Combine all ingredients in medium bowl of electric mixer, beat on low speed until ingredients are combined. Then, beat on medium speed until mixture is smooth and changed in colour. Spread mixture into prepared pan. Bake in moderate oven about 45 minutes. Stand few minutes before turning onto wire rack to cool.

Top cold cake with 1 quantity Chocolate Glace Icing (page 120) and chopped almonds, if desired.

APPLE WALNUT CAKE

125g butter, chopped
2 teaspoons grated orange rind
1 cup (220g) castor sugar
½ cup (100g) firmly packed
**   brown sugar**
2 eggs
1½ cups (225g) self-raising flour
½ cup (75g) plain flour
½ teaspoon bicarbonate of soda
1 cup (250ml) evaporated milk
1 large (200g) apple, peeled, chopped
½ cup (60g) chopped walnuts

Grease 23cm square slab cake pan, cover base with baking paper.

Combine butter, rind, sugars, eggs, flours, soda and milk in medium bowl of electric mixer, beat on low speed until ingredients are combined. Then, beat on medium speed until mixture is smooth and changed in colour. Stir in apple and nuts. Spread mixture into prepared pan. Bake in moderate oven about 55 minutes. Stand 5 minutes before turning onto wire rack to cool.

Top cold cake with 1 quantity Citrus Frosting (page 121) and sprinkle with extra walnuts, if desired.

WALNUT AND RAISIN APPLE CAKE

60g butter, chopped
1¼ cups (250g) firmly packed
**   brown sugar**
3 eggs
¾ cup (110g) plain flour
½ cup (75g) self-raising flour
1 teaspoon ground cinnamon
2 medium (300g) apples,
**   peeled, grated**
1 cup (120g) chopped walnuts
½ cup (85g) chopped raisins

Grease 15cm x 25cm loaf pan, cover base with baking paper.

Combine butter, sugar, eggs, flours and cinnamon in medium bowl of electric mixer, beat on low speed until ingredients are combined. Then, beat on medium speed until mixture is smooth and changed in colour. Stir in apples, nuts and raisins. Spoon and spread into prepared pan. Bake in moderate oven about 1¼ hours. Stand 10 minutes before turning onto wire rack to cool.

BELOW: From left: Walnut and Raisin Apple Cake, Apple Walnut Cake.

Platters and jar from Windsor Antique Market.

SPICY SPONGE CAKE

3 eggs
¾ cup (165g) castor sugar
1½ cups (225g) self-raising flour
1 teaspoon ground cinnamon
1 teaspoon ground ginger
1 teaspoon ground cloves
1 teaspoon ground cardamom
125g butter, melted
⅓ cup (80ml) milk

Grease 15cm x 25cm loaf pan, cover base with baking paper.

Beat eggs and sugar in small bowl of electric mixer on high speed about 10 minutes or until mixture is thick and creamy. Gently fold in remaining ingredients. Pour mixture into prepared pan. Bake in moderate oven about 40 minutes. Turn onto wire rack to cool.

If desired, top cold cake with 1 quantity Honey Cream Cheese Frosting (page 121) combined with 1 teaspoon finely grated lemon rind, and sprinkled lightly with orange shreds (page 123).

ABOVE: Spicy Sponge Cake.

Silver serving basket from Sydney Antique Centre; cake server from Whitehill Silver and Plate Co. Pty Ltd.

9

FUDGY CHOCOLATE CAKE

185g butter, chopped
1½ cups (330g) castor sugar
3 eggs
1½ cups (225g) self-raising flour
¾ cup (110g) plain flour
½ cup (50g) cocoa
1 cup (250ml) water

Grease deep 23cm round cake pan, line base and side with baking paper.

Combine all ingredients in medium bowl of electric mixer, beat on low speed until ingredients are combined. Then, beat on medium speed until mixture is smooth and changed in colour. Spread mixture into prepared pan. Bake in moderate oven about 1¼ hours. Stand cake 5 minutes before turning onto wire rack to cool.

If desired, split and fill cold cake with whipped cream and top with 1 quantity Chocolate Butter Cream (page 120) and chocolate curls (page 122).

CHERRY ALMOND CAKE

185g butter, chopped
¾ cup (165g) castor sugar
3 eggs
2 cups (300g) self-raising flour
2 tablespoons ground almonds
¼ cup (60ml) milk
1 cup (210g) glace cherries

Grease deep 20cm round cake pan, cover base with baking paper.

Combine butter, sugar, eggs, flour, nuts and milk in medium bowl of electric mixer, beat on low speed until ingredients are combined. Then, beat on medium speed until mixture is smooth and changed in colour. Stir in cherries. Spread mixture into prepared pan. Bake in moderate oven about 1 hour. Stand 10 minutes before turning onto wire rack to cool.

Dust cold cake with sifted icing sugar, if desired.

ABOVE: Fudgy Chocolate Cake.
RIGHT: Cherry Almond Cake.

Above: China from Limoges. Right: China from Mikasa; tray, silk flowers and embroidered cushion from Home & Garden on the Mall.

WALNUT BUTTER CAKE

125g butter, chopped
1 cup (220g) castor sugar
3 eggs
1 cup (150g) self-raising flour
¼ cup (35g) plain flour
¼ cup (60ml) milk
2 cups (240g) chopped walnuts

Grease 23cm square slab cake pan, cover base with baking paper.

Combine butter, sugar, eggs, flours and milk in medium bowl of electric mixer, beat on low speed until ingredients are combined. Then, beat on medium speed until mixture is smooth and changed in colour. Stir in nuts. Spread mixture into prepared pan. Bake in moderate oven about 40 minutes. Turn onto wire rack to cool.

If desired, split cold cake, fill with whipped cream, top with 1 quantity Rich Chocolate Glace Icing (page 120) and sprinkle with extra chopped walnuts.

BUTTER ALMOND CAKE

250g butter, chopped
½ teaspoon almond essence
1 cup (220g) castor sugar
4 eggs
⅔ cup (80g) packaged
 ground almonds
1 cup (150g) plain flour
¾ cup (110g) self-raising flour
¼ cup (60ml) milk
⅓ cup (25g) flaked almonds

Grease deep 20cm round cake pan, cover base with baking paper.

Combine butter, essence, sugar, eggs, ground almonds, flours and milk in medium bowl of electric mixer, beat on low speed until ingredients are combined. Then, beat on medium speed until mixture is smooth and changed in colour. Spread mixture into prepared pan, sprinkle with flaked almonds. Bake in moderately slow oven about 1¼ hours. Stand 5 minutes before turning onto wire rack to cool.

HAZELNUT BUTTER CAKE

125g butter, chopped
1 teaspoon vanilla essence
1 cup (220g) castor sugar
2 eggs
1½ cups (225g) self-raising flour
¾ cup (180ml) milk
⅔ cup (70g) packaged ground
 hazelnuts

Grease deep 20cm round cake pan, cover base with baking paper.

Combine butter, essence, sugar, eggs, flour and milk in medium bowl of electric mixer, beat on low speed until ingredients are combined. Then, beat on medium speed until mixture is smooth and changed in colour. Stir in nuts. Pour mixture into prepared pan. Bake in moderate oven about 50 minutes. Turn onto wire rack to cool.

If desired, split cold cake into 3 layers, sandwich layers with 1 quantity Chocolate Liqueur Cream (page 121), top with 1 quantity Rich Chocolate Glace Icing (page 120) and decorate with chocolate lace (page 122).

MOIST CARROT AND GINGER LOAF

You will need about 250g carrots for this loaf.

1 cup (200g) firmly packed
 brown sugar
2 eggs
⅔ cup (160ml) vegetable oil
1 cup (150g) self-raising flour
1 teaspoon bicarbonate of soda
1½ cups coarsely grated carrot
½ cup (80g) sultanas
½ cup (100g) chopped glace ginger
½ cup (60g) chopped walnuts

Grease 15cm x 25cm loaf pan, cover base with baking paper.

Combine sugar, eggs, oil, flour and soda in medium bowl of electric mixer, beat on low speed until ingredients are combined. Then, beat on medium speed until mixture is smooth and changed in colour. Stir in carrot, sultanas, ginger and nuts. Pour mixture into prepared pan. Bake in moderately slow oven about 1 hour. Turn onto wire rack to cool.

Top cold cake with 1 quantity Cream Cheese Frosting (page 121), if desired.

LEFT: Clockwise from back: Hazelnut Butter Cake, Butter Almond Cake, Walnut Butter Cake.
RIGHT: Moist Carrot and Ginger Loaf.

Left: China from Accoutrement. Right: Canisters, plate and tin from Windsor Antique Market; fabric from Les Olivades.

CHOCOLATE BAR CAKE

90g butter, chopped
½ cup (110g) castor sugar
2 eggs
½ cup (75g) self-raising flour
2 tablespoons cocoa

Grease 8cm x 26cm bar cake pan, cover base with baking paper.

Combine all ingredients in small bowl of electric mixer, beat on low speed until ingredients are combined. Then, beat on medium speed until mixture is smooth and changed in colour. Spread mixture into prepared pan. Bake in moderate oven about 35 minutes. Stand few minutes before turning onto wire rack to cool.

If desired, split cold cake into 3 layers, fill and decorate with whipped cream, grated chocolate and strawberries.

WHOLEMEAL BANANA COCONUT CAKE

You will need about 2 over-ripe medium bananas for this cake.

125g butter, chopped
2 teaspoons grated lemon rind
⅔ cup (130g) firmly packed
  brown sugar
3 eggs
¾ cup mashed banana
⅓ cup (30g) coconut
¾ cup (110g) white self-raising flour
¾ cup (120g) wholemeal
  self-raising flour
1 teaspoon bicarbonate of soda

Coat 21cm baba cake pan with non-stick spray. Combine all ingredients in medium bowl of electric mixer, beat on low speed until ingredients are combined. Then, beat on medium speed until mixture is smooth and changed in colour. Spoon and spread mixture into prepared pan. Bake in moderate oven about 45 minutes. Turn onto wire rack to cool.

Top cold cake with 1 quantity Lemon Glace Icing (page 120) and toasted flaked coconut (page 122), if desired.

FAMILY-SIZED BANANA CAKE

You will need about 5 over-ripe medium bananas for this cake.

1 cup (250ml) vegetable oil
1⅓ cups (295g) castor sugar
4 eggs
2¾ cups (410g) self-raising flour
1 teaspoon bicarbonate of soda
2 cups mashed banana

Grease deep 23cm square cake pan, cover base with baking paper.

Combine all ingredients in large bowl of electric mixer, beat on low speed until ingredients are combined. Then, beat on medium speed until mixture is smooth and changed in colour. Pour mixture into prepared pan. Bake in moderately slow oven about 1¼ hours. Stand 5 minutes before turning onto wire rack to cool.

Top cold cake with 1 quantity Caramel Icing (page 120) and pecans, if desired.

BELOW: Chocolate Bar Cake.
RIGHT: From left: Family-Sized Banana Cake, Wholemeal Banana Coconut Cake.

Below: China from Royal Doulton. Right: China from Villeroy & Boch.

VANILLA SAND CAKE

185g butter, chopped
1 teaspoon vanilla essence
¾ cup (165g) castor sugar
3 eggs
½ cup (75g) self-raising flour
⅓ cup (50g) arrowroot
⅓ cup (50g) rice flour

Coat 21cm baba cake pan with non-stick spray. Combine all ingredients in medium bowl of electric mixer, beat on low speed until ingredients are combined. Then, beat on medium speed until mixture is smooth and changed in colour. Spoon and spread mixture into prepared pan. Bake in moderate oven about 45 minutes. Turn onto wire rack to cool.

Dust cold cake with sifted icing sugar, if desired.

ABOVE: Vanilla Sand Cake.
ABOVE RIGHT: Soft 'n' Spicy Treacle Gingerbread.
RIGHT: Hazelnut Choc-Apple Cake.

Above right: Rug, coffee cups, jug and plate from Butler & Co. Right: Glass dishes from Windsor Antique Market.

HAZELNUT CHOC-APPLE CAKE

185g butter, chopped
¾ cup (165g) castor sugar
3 eggs
½ cup (75g) self-raising flour
2 tablespoons cocoa
1¾ cups (190g) packaged
  ground hazelnuts
1 large (200g) apple, peeled, grated

Grease deep 20cm round cake pan, line base and side with baking paper.

Combine butter, sugar, eggs, flour and cocoa in medium bowl of electric mixer, beat on low speed until ingredients are combined. Then, beat on medium speed until mixture is smooth and changed in colour. Stir in nuts and apple. Spread mixture into prepared pan. Bake in moderately slow oven about 1¼ hours. Stand 5 minutes before turning onto wire rack to cool.

Top cold cake wth 1 quantity Chocolate Butter Cream (page120) and chopped hazelnuts, if desired.

SOFT 'N' SPICY TREACLE GINGERBREAD

250g butter, chopped
1 cup (200g) firmly packed
   brown sugar
2 eggs
3 cups (450g) plain flour
2 teaspoons bicarbonate of soda
1 tablespoon ground ginger
1 tablespoon ground cinnamon
1 teaspoon ground allspice
¾ cup (180ml) treacle
1 cup (250ml) buttermilk

Grease deep 23cm square cake pan, cover base with baking paper.

Combine all ingredients in large bowl of electric mixer, beat on low speed until ingredients are combined. Then, beat on medium speed until mixture is smooth and changed in colour. Spoon and spread mixture into prepared pan. Bake in moderately slow oven about 1½ hours. Stand 10 minutes before turning onto wire rack to cool.

Top cold cake with 2 quantities Chocolate Glace Icing (page 120) and chopped glace ginger, if desired.

CHOCOLATE MAYONNAISE CAKE

2 cups (300g) self-raising flour
1 cup (220g) castor sugar
⅓ cup (35g) cocoa
1 cup (250ml) water
⅔ cup (160ml) bottled whole
  egg mayonnaise

Grease deep 20cm round cake pan, cover base with baking paper.

Combine all ingredients in medium bowl of electric mixer, beat on low speed until ingredients are combined. Then, beat on medium speed until mixture is smooth and changed in colour. Pour mixture into prepared pan. Bake in moderately slow oven about 1 hour 10 minutes. Stand few minutes before turning onto wire rack to cool.

If desired, make 1½ quantities Chocolate Butter Cream (page 120). Spread side of cold cake with some of the butter cream, roll in crushed nuts. Spread top with more butter cream and decorate with white chocolate curls (page 122).

RICH SULTANA CHERRY CAKE

250g butter, chopped
1 cup (220g) castor sugar
5 eggs
1¼ cups (185g) plain flour
½ cup (75g) self-raising flour
4½ cups (750g) sultanas
½ cup (125g) chopped glace cherries

Line base and sides of deep 19cm square cake pan with 3 layers of baking paper, bringing paper 5cm above edges of pan.

Combine butter, sugar, eggs and flours in large bowl of electric mixer, beat on low speed until ingredients are combined. Then, beat on medium speed until mixture is smooth and changed in colour. Stir in sultanas and cherries. Spoon and spread mixture into prepared pan. Bake in slow oven about 2¼ hours. Cover hot cake tightly with foil, cool in pan.

PINEAPPLE, RUM AND CHERRY CAKE

250g butter, chopped
2 teaspoons grated lemon rind
1 tablespoon grated orange rind
1 cup (220g) castor sugar
4 eggs
1¾ cups (260g) plain flour
¼ cup (35g) self-raising flour
2 tablespoons dark rum
1 cup (250g) chopped glace cherries
¾ cup (170g) chopped
  glace pineapple
1 cup (160g) sultanas

Grease deep 20cm round cake pan, line base and side with baking paper.

Combine butter, rinds, sugar, eggs, flours and rum in large bowl of electric mixer, beat on low speed until ingredients are combined. Then, beat on medium speed until mixture is smooth and changed in colour. Stir in fruit, spread mixture into prepared pan. Bake in moderately slow oven about 2 hours. Cover hot cake tightly with foil, cool in pan.

RIGHT: From left: Rich Sultana Cherry Cake, Pineapple, Rum and Cherry Cake.
BELOW: Chocolate Mayonnaise Cake.

Below: China from Mikasa Tableware.

FAMILY-SIZED BUTTERY VANILLA CAKE

250g butter, chopped
2 teaspoons vanilla essence
2 cups (440g) castor sugar
4 eggs
2 cups (300g) self-raising flour
⅓ cup (40g) custard powder
1 cup (250ml) milk

Grease deep 23cm square cake pan, line base and sides with baking paper.

Combine all ingredients in large bowl of electric mixer, beat on low speed until ingredients are combined. Then, beat on medium speed until mixture is smooth and changed in colour. Spread into prepared pan. Bake in moderately slow oven about 1¼ hours. Stand 5 minutes before turning onto wire rack to cool.

Dust cold cake with sifted icing sugar, if desired.

BELOW: Family-Sized Buttery Vanilla Cake.

China from Villeroy & Boch; basket and napery from Accoutrement.

MOCHA SOUR CREAM CAKE

125g dark chocolate, melted
125g butter, chopped
⅔ cup (150g) castor sugar
2 eggs
1¼ cups (185g) self-raising flour
1 tablespoon instant coffee powder
½ cup (125ml) sour cream

Grease 14cm x 21cm loaf pan, cover base with baking paper.

Combine all ingredients in medium bowl of electric mixer, beat on low speed until ingredients are combined. Then, beat on medium speed until mixture is just smooth and changed in colour; do not over-beat. Spread mixture into prepared pan. Bake in moderate oven about 1 hour. Stand few minutes before turning onto wire rack to cool.

Top cold cake with 1 quantity Coffee Vienna Cream Frosting (page 121), if desired.

MOCHA YOGURT CAKE

60g butter, chopped
1 cup (220g) castor sugar
2 eggs
1½ cups (225g) self-raising flour
⅓ cup (35g) cocoa
2 teaspoons instant coffee powder
1 teaspoon bicarbonate of soda
1 cup (250ml) plain yogurt

Grease 21cm baba cake pan. Combine all ingredients in medium bowl of electric mixer, beat on low speed until ingredients are combined. Then, beat on medium speed until mixture is smooth and changed in colour. Spoon mixture into prepared pan. Bake in moderate oven about 50 minutes. Stand few minutes before turning onto wire rack to cool.

Drizzle cold cake with 1 quantity Coffee Glace Icing (page 120) and decorate with walnuts, if desired.

RIGHT: From left: Mocha Sour Cream Cake, Mocha Yogurt Cake.

China is Spode by Waterford Wedgwood.

WHOLEMEAL BRAN BANANA CAKE

You will need about 2 over-ripe medium bananas for this cake.

125g butter, chopped
1 cup (200g) firmly packed brown sugar
3 eggs
1½ cups (240g) wholemeal self-raising flour
¼ cup (20g) unprocessed bran
⅓ cup (30g) coconut
⅔ cup mashed banana
½ cup (125ml) milk

Grease 15cm x 25cm loaf pan, cover base with baking paper.

Combine all ingredients in medium bowl of electric mixer, beat on low speed until ingredients are combined. Then, beat on medium speed until mixture is smooth and changed in colour. Spread mixture into prepared pan. Bake in moderate oven about 1 hour 10 minutes. Turn onto wire rack to cool.

MOIST BANANA LOAF

You will need about 4 over-ripe medium bananas for this loaf.

125g butter, chopped
1 teaspoon vanilla essence
½ cup (110g) castor sugar
2 eggs
1½ cups mashed banana
1½ cups (225g) self-raising flour
1 teaspoon bicarbonate of soda
1 tablespoon milk

Grease 14cm x 21cm loaf pan, cover base with baking paper.

Combine all ingredients in medium bowl of electric mixer, beat on low speed until ingredients are combined. Then, beat on medium speed until mixture is smooth and changed in colour. Spread mixture into prepared pan. Bake in moderate oven about 1 hour. Turn onto wire rack to cool.

Top cold cake with 1 quantity Citrus Frosting (page 121) and sliced banana dipped in lemon juice, if desired.

BUTTERY BANANA CAKE

You will need about 3 over-ripe medium bananas for this cake.

250g butter, chopped
1 cup (220g) castor sugar
3 eggs
2 cups (300g) self-raising flour
1 cup mashed banana

Grease 23cm square slab cake pan, cover base with baking paper.

Combine all ingredients in medium bowl of electric mixer, beat on low speed until ingredients are combined. Then, beat on medium speed until mixture is smooth and changed in colour. Spoon and spread mixture into prepared pan. Bake in moderate oven about 45 minutes. Stand 5 minutes before turning onto wire rack to cool.

Top cold cake with 2 quantities Passion-fruit Glace Icing (page 120), if desired.

GOLDEN GINGER SULTANA CAKE

125g butter, chopped
½ cup (100g) firmly packed
    brown sugar
2 eggs
2 cups (300g) plain flour
1 teaspoon ground ginger
1 cup (250ml) golden syrup
½ cup (125ml) milk
½ teaspoon bicarbonate of soda
½ cup (80g) sultanas
⅓ cup (60g) glace ginger, chopped

Grease 20cm x 30cm lamington pan, cover base with baking paper.

Combine butter, sugar, eggs, flour, ground ginger, golden syrup, milk and soda in medium bowl of electric mixer, beat on low speed until ingredients are combined. Then, beat on medium speed until mixture is smooth and changed in colour. Stir in sultanas and glace ginger. Spread mixture into prepared pan. Bake in moderately slow oven about 55 minutes. Turn onto wire rack to cool.

Top cold cake with 1 quantity Cinnamon Vienna Cream Frosting (page 121), if desired.

MOLASSES WHOLEMEAL GINGERBREAD

125g butter, chopped
1 cup (220g) raw sugar
2 eggs
½ cup (125ml) molasses
1⅓ cups (200g) wholemeal plain flour
1 cup (160g) wholemeal
    self-raising flour
1 teaspoon ground ginger
½ teaspoon ground cinnamon
½ teaspoon ground nutmeg
¾ cup (180ml) hot water

Grease 14cm x 21cm loaf pan, cover base with baking paper.

Combine all ingredients in medium bowl of electric mixer, beat on low speed until ingredients are combined. Then, beat on medium speed until mixture is smooth and changed in colour. Spoon and spread mixture into prepared pan. Bake in moderate oven about 1½ hours. Turn onto wire rack to cool.

LEFT: Clockwise from back: Buttery Banana Cake, Wholemeal Bran Banana Cake, Moist Banana Loaf.
RIGHT: From back: Golden Ginger Sultana Cake, Molasses Wholemeal Gingerbread.

Left: China and cake server from Royal Doulton.
Right: China from Villeroy & Boch.

MOIST GINGER CAKE

125g butter, chopped
125g packet cream cheese, chopped
1¼ cups (250g) firmly packed
  brown sugar
2 eggs
1½ cups (225g) self-raising flour
1 tablespoon ground ginger
1 teaspoon ground cinnamon
2 tablespoons golden syrup
1 tablespoon treacle

Grease 23cm square slab cake pan, cover base with baking paper.

Combine all ingredients in medium bowl of electric mixer, beat on low speed until ingredients are combined. Then, beat on medium speed until mixture is smooth and changed in colour. Spread mixture into prepared pan. Bake in moderate oven about 40 minutes. Turn onto wire rack to cool.

Top cold cake with 1 quantity Golden Cream Cheese Frosting (page 121) and sprinkle with chopped glace ginger, if desired.

CUT 'N' KEEP BUTTER CAKE

125g butter, chopped
1¼ cups (275g) castor sugar
3 eggs
1 cup (150g) plain flour
½ cup (75g) self-raising flour
¼ teaspoon bicarbonate of soda
½ cup (125ml) milk

Grease deep 20cm round cake pan, cover base with baking paper.

Combine all ingredients in medium bowl of electric mixer, beat on low speed until ingredients are combined. Then, beat on medium speed until mixture is smooth and changed in colour. Spread into prepared pan. Bake in moderately slow oven about 1¼ hours. Stand few minutes before turning onto wire rack to cool.

Top cold cake with 1 quantity pink Vienna Cream Frosting (page 121) and maraschino cherries, if desired.

CREAM CHEESE LEMON CAKE

125g butter, chopped
125g packet cream cheese, chopped
3 teaspoons grated lemon rind
1 cup (220g) castor sugar
2 eggs
¾ cup (110g) self-raising flour
½ cup (75g) plain flour

Grease 21cm baba cake pan. Combine all ingredients in medium bowl of electric mixer, beat on low speed until all ingredients are combined. Then, beat on medium speed until mixture is smooth and changed in colour. Spoon and spread mixture into prepared pan. Bake in moderately slow oven about 55 minutes. Stand few minutes before turning onto wire rack to cool.

Dust cold cake with sifted icing sugar, if desired.

BELOW: Moist Ginger Cake.
RIGHT: From back: Cut 'n' Keep Butter Cake, Cream Cheese Lemon Cake.

Below: China from Royal Doulton; board and serviette from Appley Hoare Antiques.

SUPER-FINE CHOCOLATE CAKE

125g butter, chopped
1¼ cups (275g) castor sugar
2 eggs
1¾ cups (260g) self-raising flour
½ teaspoon bicarbonate of soda
½ cup (50g) cocoa
½ cup (125ml) milk

Grease 21cm baba cake pan. Combine all ingredients in medium bowl of electric mixer, beat on low speed until ingredients are combined. Then, beat on medium speed until mixture is smooth and changed in colour. Spread mixture into prepared pan. Bake in moderate oven about 1 hour. Turn onto wire rack to cool.

Drizzle cold cake with 1 quantity Chocolate Glace Icing (page 120), if desired.

LEFT: From back: Chocolate Layer Cake, Super-Fine Chocolate Cake.
BELOW: Lemon Delicious Cake.

Left: China from Royal Doulton. Below: China from Royal Albert.

CHOCOLATE LAYER CAKE

150g butter, chopped
1 cup (220g) castor sugar
3 eggs
1½ cups (225g) self-raising flour
½ cup (75g) plain flour
⅓ cup (35g) cocoa
½ teaspoon bicarbonate of soda
½ cup (125ml) milk

Grease deep 20cm round cake pan, cover base with baking paper.

Combine all ingredients in medium bowl of electric mixer, beat on low speed until ingredients are combined. Then, beat on medium speed until mixture is smooth and changed in colour. Spoon and spread mixture into prepared pan. Bake in moderate oven about 1 hour 10 minutes. Stand 5 minutes before turning onto wire rack to cool.

If desired, make 1½ quantities Chocolate Butter Cream (page 120). Split cold cake into 3 layers, sandwich with some of the butter cream, whipped cream and sliced strawberries. Spread cake all over with remaining butter cream and decorate with white chocolate curls (page 122).

LEMON DELICIOUS CAKE

125g butter, chopped
2 teaspoons grated lemon rind
1¼ cups (275g) castor sugar
3 eggs
½ cup (125ml) milk
1½ cups (225g) self-raising flour
¼ cup (60ml) lemon juice

Coat 21cm baba cake pan with non-stick spray. Combine all ingredients in medium bowl of electric mixer, beat on low speed until ingredients are combined. Then, beat on medium speed until mixture is smooth and changed in colour. Pour and spread mixture into prepared pan. Bake in moderate oven about 50 minutes. Turn onto wire rack to cool.

Dust cold cake with sifted icing sugar, if desired.

MOIST BANANA CAKE

You will need about 4 over-ripe medium bananas for this cake.

125g butter, chopped
1 teaspoon vanilla essence
¾ cup (165g) castor sugar
2 eggs
1½ cups (240g) wholemeal
    self-raising flour
½ teaspoon bicarbonate of soda
1⅔ cups mashed banana
2 tablespoons milk

Coat 21cm baba cake pan with non-stick spray. Combine all ingredients in medium bowl of electric mixer, beat on low speed until ingredients are combined. Then, beat on medium speed until mixture is smooth and changed in colour. Pour and spread mixture into prepared pan. Bake in moderate oven about 50 minutes. Turn onto wire rack to cool.

SOUR CREAM BANANA CAKE

You will need about 3 over-ripe medium bananas for this cake.

125g butter, chopped
¾ cup (150g) firmly packed
    brown sugar
2 eggs
1½ cups (225g) self-raising flour
1 teaspoon bicarbonate of soda
1 cup mashed banana
⅔ cup (160ml) sour cream

WHOLEMEAL CHOCOLATE FUDGE CAKE

125g butter, chopped
1 cup (220g) castor sugar
2 eggs
1½ cups (240g) wholemeal
   self-raising flour
⅔ cup (75g) cocoa
1 cup (250ml) milk
2 teaspoons white vinegar
½ cup (125ml) hot water

Grease 15cm x 25cm loaf pan, cover base with baking paper.

Combine all ingredients in medium bowl of electric mixer, beat on low speed until ingredients are combined. Then, beat on medium speed until mixture is smooth and changed in colour. Pour mixture into prepared pan. Bake in moderately slow oven about 1¼ hours. Turn onto wire rack to cool.

Top cold cake with 1 quantity Honey Cream Cheese Frosting (page 121) marbled with ½ quantity Chocolate Butter Cream (page 120), if desired.

LEFT: From left: Moist Banana Cake, Sour Cream Banana Cake.
BELOW: Wholemeal Chocolate Fudge Cake.

Left: China from Villeroy & Boch. Below: China from Royal Doulton.

Coat 21cm baba cake pan with non-stick spray. Combine all ingredients in medium bowl of electric mixer, beat on low speed until ingredients are combined. Then, beat on medium speed until mixture is smooth and changed in colour. Spoon and spread mixture into prepared pan. Bake in moderate oven about 45 minutes. Stand few minutes before turning onto wire rack to cool.

Drizzle cold cake with 1 quantity Lemon Glace Icing (page 120), if desired.

LIGHT GINGER CAKE

125g butter, chopped
½ cup (100g) firmly packed
 brown sugar
2 eggs
2 cups (300g) plain flour
½ teaspoon bicarbonate of soda
1 teaspoon ground ginger
1 cup (250ml) golden syrup
½ cup (125ml) milk

Coat 21cm baba cake pan with non-stick spray. Combine all ingredients in medium bowl of electric mixer, beat on low speed until ingredients are combined. Then, beat on medium speed until mixture is smooth and changed in colour. Spread mixture into prepared pan. Bake in moderate oven about 50 minutes. Stand 5 minutes before turning onto wire rack to cool.

Drizzle cold cake with 1 quantity Chocolate Glace Icing (page 120), if desired.

MAPLE SYRUP CAKE

185g butter, chopped
¾ cup (150g) firmly packed
 brown sugar
⅓ cup (80ml) maple syrup
2 eggs
1½ cups (225g) self-raising flour
½ cup (75g) plain flour
½ cup (125ml) milk

Coat 21cm baba cake pan with non-stick spray. Combine all ingredients in medium bowl of electric mixer, beat on low speed until ingredients are combined. Then, beat on medium speed until mixture is smooth and changed in colour. Spread mixture into prepared pan. Bake in

moderate oven about 45 minutes. Stand 5 minutes before turning onto wire rack to cool.

Top cold cake with 1 quantity Maple Syrup Glace Icing (page 120), if desired.

SPICY GOLDEN GINGER CAKE

125g butter, chopped
½ cup (110g) castor sugar
1 egg
1 cup (250ml) golden syrup
2 cups (300g) plain flour
½ cup (75g) self-raising flour
3 teaspoons ground ginger
1 teaspoon ground cinnamon
½ teaspoon ground cloves
1 teaspoon bicarbonate of soda
1 cup (250ml) hot water

Grease deep 23cm round cake pan, cover base with baking paper.

Combine all ingredients in medium bowl of electric mixer, beat on low speed until ingredients are combined. Then, beat on medium speed until mixture is smooth and changed in colour. Pour mixture into prepared pan. Bake in moderately slow oven about 1¼ hours. Stand 10 minutes before turning onto wire rack to cool.

Top cold cake with 1 quantity Citrus Frosting (page 121) combined with 1 tablespoon chopped glace ginger, if desired.

RIGHT: From left: Spicy Golden Ginger Cake, Light Ginger Cake.
BELOW: Maple Syrup Cake.

Right: Serviette from Between the Sheets.

APPLE APRICOT SURPRISE CAKE

125g butter, chopped
¾ cup (165g) castor sugar
2 eggs
¾ cup (110g) plain flour
½ cup (75g) self-raising flour
¼ cup (60ml) milk
½ cup (125g) canned pie apples
1 tablespoon apricot jam

Grease 21cm baba cake pan. Combine butter, sugar, eggs, flours and milk in small bowl of electric mixer, beat on low speed until ingredients are combined. Then, beat on medium speed until mixture is smooth and changed in colour. Spread two-thirds of the mixture into prepared pan, top with apple and jam, spread with remaining mixture. Bake in moderate oven about 40 minutes. Stand few minutes before turning onto wire rack to cool.

Dust cold cake with sifted icing sugar, if desired.

COCONUT SPONGE CAKE

185g butter, chopped
¾ cup (165g) castor sugar
3 eggs
⅔ cup (60g) coconut
1½ cups (225g) self-raising flour
1 teaspoon baking powder
⅓ cup (80ml) milk

Grease 20cm x 30cm lamington pan, cover base with baking paper.

Combine all ingredients in medium bowl of electric mixer, beat on low speed until ingredients are combined. Then, beat on medium speed until mixture is smooth and changed in colour. Spread mixture into prepared pan. Bake in moderate oven about 30 minutes. Turn onto wire rack to cool.

If desired, split cold cake and fill with 1 quantity Passionfruit Cream (page 121), and top with Passionfruit Glace Icing (page 120).

ABOVE: From left: Apple Apricot Surprise Cake, Coconut Sponge Cake.
ABOVE RIGHT: Light Banana Buttermilk Cake.
RIGHT: Light Fruit Cake.

Above right: Tray and cloth from Between the Sheets.

LIGHT FRUIT CAKE

185g butter, chopped
⅔ cup (130g) firmly packed
   brown sugar
4 eggs
1½ cups (225g) plain flour
½ cup (75g) self-raising flour
⅓ cup (80ml) milk
2¾ cups (500g) mixed dried fruit
¾ cup (125g) mixed peel
½ cup (125g) glace cherries, halved
½ cup (70g) slivered almonds

Line base and side of deep 20cm round cake pan with 3 layers of baking paper, bringing paper 5cm above edge of pan.

Combine butter, sugar, eggs, flours and milk in medium bowl of electric mixer, beat on low speed until ingredients are combined. Then, beat on medium speed until mixture is smooth and changed in colour. Stir in fruit, peel and cherries, spoon into prepared pan, sprinkle with nuts. Bake in slow oven about 2¼ hours. Cover hot cake tightly with foil, cool in pan.

LIGHT BANANA BUTTERMILK CAKE

You will need about 1 over-ripe medium banana for this cake.

90g butter, chopped
⅔ cup (130g) firmly packed
   brown sugar
1 egg
1¼ cups (185g) self-raising flour
½ teaspoon bicarbonate of soda
½ cup mashed banana
⅓ cup (80ml) buttermilk
⅓ cup (40g) walnuts,
   coarsely chopped

Grease 20cm ring cake pan. Combine butter, sugar, egg, flour, soda, banana and buttermilk in small bowl of electric mixer, beat on low speed until ingredients are combined. Then, beat on medium speed until mixture is smooth and changed in colour. Stir in nuts. Pour into prepared pan. Bake in moderate oven about 35 minutes. Turn onto wire rack to cool.

Top cold cake with 1 quantity Lemon Glace Icing (page 120) and extra chopped walnuts, if desired.

PUMPKIN CHOC-ORANGE CAKE

You will need to cook about 300g peeled, seeded pumpkin for this cake.

125g butter, chopped
1 tablespoon grated orange rind
½ cup (100g) firmly packed
  brown sugar
1 egg
1¼ cups (185g) self-raising flour
1 tablespoon custard powder
2 tablespoons cocoa
1 teaspoon bicarbonate of soda
¾ cup cold cooked mashed pumpkin
1 tablespoon golden syrup
¼ cup (60ml) orange juice

Grease 14cm x 21cm loaf pan, cover base with baking paper.

Combine all ingredients in medium bowl of electric mixer, beat on low speed until ingredients are combined. Then, beat on medium speed until mixture is smooth and changed in colour. Spoon and spread mixture into prepared pan. Bake in moderate oven about 55 minutes. Stand 10 minutes before turning onto wire rack to cool.

Top cold cake with 1 quantity Citrus Frosting (page 121) and orange shreds (page 123), if desired.

COCONUT PUMPKIN CAKE

You will need to cook about 400g peeled, seeded pumpkin for this cake.

125g butter, chopped
2 teaspoons grated orange rind
1 cup (220g) raw sugar
3 eggs
1 cup (90g) coconut
1 cup cold cooked mashed pumpkin
1½ cups (240g) wholemeal
  self-raising flour

Grease 15cm x 25cm loaf pan, cover base with baking paper.

Combine all ingredients in medium bowl of electric mixer, beat on low speed

FLUFFY CHOCOLATE CAKE

125g butter, chopped
1 cup (220g) castor sugar
2 eggs
1½ cups (225g) self-raising flour
⅓ cup (35g) cocoa
½ teaspoon bicarbonate of soda
1 cup (250ml) water

Coat 21cm baba cake pan with non-stick spray. Combine all ingredients in medium bowl of electric mixer, beat on low speed until ingredients are combined. Then, beat on medium speed until mixture is smooth and changed in colour. Pour mixture into prepared pan, bake in moderate oven about 50 minutes. Stand 5 minutes before turning onto wire rack to cool.

Dust cold cake with equal quantities sifted icing sugar and cocoa, if desired.

until ingredients are combined. Then, beat on medium speed until mixture is smooth and changed in colour. Spread mixture into prepared pan. Bake in moderate oven about 1 hour 10 minutes. Stand 5 minutes before turning onto wire rack to cool.

Dust cold cake with sifted icing sugar, if desired.

ABOVE: From left: Coconut Pumpkin Cake, Pumpkin Choc-Orange Cake.
RIGHT: Fluffy Chocolate Cake.

Above: China from Country Road Homewear; basket from In House Collections.

FIG AND PECAN LOAF

185g butter, chopped
¾ cup (165g) castor sugar
3 eggs
1 cup (150g) plain flour
1 cup (150g) self-raising flour
1 teaspoon ground cinnamon
½ cup (125ml) milk
1 cup (250g) chopped glace figs
½ cup (125g) chopped glace apricots
⅓ cup (65g) Milk Bits
¾ cup (90g) chopped pecans

Grease 15cm x 25cm loaf pan, cover base with baking paper.

Combine butter, sugar, eggs, flours, cinnamon and milk in medium bowl of electric mixer, beat on low speed until ingredients are combined. Then, beat on medium speed until mixture is smooth and changed in colour. Stir in remaining ingredients. Spread mixture into prepared pan. Bake in moderately slow oven about 1½ hours. Stand 5 minutes before turning onto wire rack to cool.

Dust cold cake with sifted icing sugar, if desired.

RIGHT: Fig and Pecan Loaf.
FAR RIGHT: Cream Cheese Fruit Cake.
BELOW: Dark Chocolate Dessert Cake.

Far right: China is Spode by Waterford Wedgwood.
Below: China from Limoges; fabric from
I. Redelman & Son Pty. Ltd.

DARK CHOCOLATE DESSERT CAKE

125g butter, chopped
1½ cups (330g) castor sugar
3 eggs
1 cup (150g) plain flour
1 cup (150g) self-raising flour
¾ cup (75g) cocoa
½ cup (125ml) water
1 cup (250ml) milk

Grease deep 23cm round cake pan, cover base with baking paper.

Combine all ingredients in medium bowl of electric mixer, beat on low speed until ingredients are combined. Then, beat on medium speed until mixture is smooth and changed in colour. Pour mixture into prepared pan. Bake in moderately slow oven about 1¼ hours. Stand 5 minutes before turning onto wire rack to cool.

Top cold cake with 1 quantity Chocolate Glaze (page 120), if desired.

CREAM CHEESE FRUIT CAKE

90g butter, chopped
125g packet cream cheese, chopped
¾ cup (165g) castor sugar
2 eggs
½ cup (75g) plain flour
½ cup (75g) self-raising flour
¼ cup (60ml) brandy
1½ cups (315g) chopped
  pitted prunes
¾ cup (185g) chopped glace apricots

Line base and side of deep 20cm round cake pan with 3 layers of baking paper, bringing paper 5cm above edge of pan.

Combine butter, cheese, sugar, eggs, flours and brandy in medium bowl of electric mixer, beat on low speed until ingredients are combined. Then, beat on medium speed until mixture is smooth and changed in colour. Stir in fruit. Spoon mixture into prepared pan. Bake in slow oven about 2½ hours. Cover hot cake tightly with foil, cool in pan.

ORANGE SOUR CREAM CAKE

90g butter, chopped
1 tablespoon grated orange rind
¾ cup (165g) castor sugar
2 eggs
1 cup (150g) self-raising flour
½ cup (75g) plain flour
½ teaspoon bicarbonate of soda
½ cup (125ml) sour cream

Grease 14cm x 21cm loaf pan, cover base with baking paper.

Combine all ingredients in medium bowl of electric mixer, beat on low speed until ingredients are combined. Then, beat on medium speed until mixture is smooth and changed in colour. Spread mixture into prepared pan. Bake in moderate oven about 50 minutes. Turn onto wire rack to cool.

Top cold cake with 1 quantity Orange Vienna Cream Frosting (page 121), if desired.

DOUBLE ORANGE CAKE

125g butter, chopped
1 tablespoon grated orange rind
¾ cup (165g) castor sugar
2 eggs
1½ cups (225g) self-raising flour
⅓ cup (80ml) orange juice
½ cup (125ml) milk

Coat 21cm baba cake pan with non-stick spray. Combine all ingredients in medium bowl of electric mixer, beat on low speed until ingredients are combined. Then, beat on medium speed until mixture is smooth and changed in colour. (Mixture might appear to be curdled at this stage, but will reconstitute later.) Pour and spread mixture into prepared pan. Bake in moderate oven about 40 minutes. Stand 5 minutes before turning onto wire rack to cool.

Dust cold cake with sifted icing sugar, if desired.

DOUBLE LEMON LOAF

90g butter, chopped
1 tablespoon grated lemon rind
½ cup (110g) castor sugar
2 eggs
1¾ cups (260g) self-raising flour
¾ cup (180ml) milk
¼ cup (40g) mixed peel
¼ cup (60ml) lemon-flavoured spread

Grease 14cm x 21cm loaf pan, cover base with baking paper.

Combine butter, rind, sugar, eggs, flour and milk in medium bowl of electric mixer, beat on low speed until ingredients are combined. Then, beat on medium speed until mixture is just smooth and changed in colour; do not over-beat. Stir in peel. Spread mixture into prepared pan, drop teaspoons of lemon spread over mixture,

swirl with knife. Bake in moderate oven about 1 hour. Turn onto wire rack to cool.

LEFT: From left: Double Orange Cake, Orange Sour Cream Cake.
ABOVE: Double Lemon Loaf.

Above: China, teapot and basket from In House Collections. Left: Glassware from The Melbourne Shop.

PRUNE LOAF

60g butter, chopped
2 teaspoons grated lemon rind
¾ cup (150g) firmly packed
   brown sugar
2 eggs
1½ cups (240g) wholemeal
   self-raising flour
¾ cup (200g) cottage cheese
½ cup (105g) chopped pitted prunes

Grease 14cm x 21cm loaf pan, cover base with baking paper.

Combine butter, rind, sugar, eggs and flour in medium bowl of electric mixer, beat on low speed until ingredients are combined. Then, beat on medium speed until mixture is smooth and changed in colour. Stir in cheese and prunes. Spread mixture into prepared pan. Bake in moderate oven about 1 hour. Turn onto wire rack to cool.

YOGURT PRUNE LOAF

125g butter, chopped
2 teaspoons grated orange rind
¾ cup (165g) raw sugar
2 eggs
2 cups (320g) wholemeal
   self-raising flour
¾ cup plain yogurt
¼ cup (60ml) orange juice
1¼ cups (250g) chopped
   pitted prunes

Grease 15cm x 25cm loaf pan, cover base with baking paper.

Combine butter, rind, sugar, eggs, flour, yogurt and juice in medium bowl of electric mixer, beat on low speed until ingredients are combined. Then, beat on medium speed until mixture is smooth and changed in colour. Stir in prunes. Spread mixture into prepared pan. Bake in moderate oven about 1 hour 10 minutes. Turn onto wire rack to cool.

CINNAMON CAKE

125g butter, chopped
1 cup (220g) castor sugar
3 eggs
1 cup (150g) self-raising flour
⅓ cup (50g) plain flour
1 tablespoon ground cinnamon
¼ cup (60ml) milk

Grease deep 20cm round cake pan, cover base with baking paper.

Combine all ingredients in medium bowl of electric mixer, beat on low speed until ingredients are combined. Then, beat on medium speed until mixture is smooth and changed in colour. Spoon and spread mixture into prepared pan. Bake in moderate oven about 50 minutes. Turn onto wire rack to cool.

Top cold cake with 1 quantity Honey Cream Cheese Frosting (page 121) and decorate with hazelnuts and chocolate shavings (page 122), if desired.

MIXED SPICE CAKE

3 eggs
¾ cup (165g) castor sugar
1½ cups (225g) self-raising flour
1 teaspoon ground cinnamon
1 teaspoon ground ginger
1 teaspoon ground cloves
1 teaspoon ground cardamom
125g butter, melted
⅓ cup (80ml) milk

Grease deep 20cm round cake pan, cover base with baking paper.

Combine eggs and sugar in small bowl of electric mixer, beat on high speed until thick and creamy. Gently fold in remaining ingredients. Pour mixture into prepared pan. Bake in moderate oven about 45 minutes. Turn cake onto wire rack to cool.

If desired, split cold cake, fill and top with honey-flavoured whipped cream; sprinkle lightly with combined ground cinnamon and nutmeg.

LEFT: From left: Prune Loaf, Yogurt Prune Loaf.
BELOW: From back: Mixed Spice Cake, Cinnamon Cake.

Below: China and canisters from Old Country Furniture Antiques.

MOCHA DELIGHT CAKE

125g butter, chopped
1½ cups (330g) castor sugar
3 eggs
2 cups (300g) plain flour
½ cup (50g) cocoa
1 teaspoon bicarbonate of soda
2 teaspoons instant coffee powder
½ cup (125ml) sour cream
¾ cup (180ml) water

Grease deep 23cm round cake pan, cover base with baking paper.

Combine all ingredients in medium bowl of electric mixer, beat on low speed until all ingredients are combined. Then, beat on medium speed until mixture is smooth and changed in colour. Spread mixture into prepared pan. Bake in moderate oven about 1¼ hours. Stand 5 minutes before turning onto wire rack to cool.

Top cold cake with 1 quantity Sour Cream Chocolate Glaze (page 121), chocolate curls (page 122) and strawberries, if desired.

BELOW: Mocha Delight Cake.

China from Limoges.

WHOLEMEAL HONEY LEMON CAKE

375g butter, chopped
1 tablespoon grated lemon rind
1¼ cups (275g) raw sugar
2 tablespoons honey
4 eggs
¾ cup (120g) wholemeal plain flour
¾ cup (110g) white self-raising flour

Grease deep 23cm round cake pan, cover base and side with baking paper, bringing paper 5cm above edge of pan.

Combine all ingredients in medium bowl of electric mixer, beat on low speed until ingredients are combined. Then, beat on medium speed until mixture is smooth and changed in colour. Spoon and spread mixture into prepared pan. Bake in moderately slow oven about 1¼ hours. Stand 10 minutes before turning onto wire rack to cool.

Dust cold cake with sifted icing sugar, if desired.

RIGHT: From left: Honeyed Date and Walnut Cake, Wholemeal Honey Lemon Cake.

China from Corso de Fiori; wire rack from In House Collections.

HONEYED DATE AND WALNUT CAKE

125g butter, chopped
½ cup (110g) castor sugar
2 tablespoons honey
2 eggs
1½ cups (225g) self-raising flour
2 teaspoons cocoa
1 teaspoon ground cinnamon
½ cup (125ml) milk
½ cup (60g) chopped walnuts
¾ cup (120g) chopped pitted dates

Coat 21cm baba cake pan with non-stick spray. Combine butter, sugar, honey, eggs, flour, cocoa, cinnamon and milk in medium bowl of electric mixer, beat on low speed until ingredients are combined. Then, beat on medium speed until mixture is smooth and changed in colour. Stir in nuts and dates. Spread mixture into prepared pan. Bake in moderate oven about 45 minutes. Turn onto wire rack to cool.

Drizzle cold cake with 1 quantity Chocolate Glace Icing (page 120) and sprinkle with extra chopped walnuts, if desired.

CHOCOLATE VELVET CAKE

125g butter, chopped
1 cup (200g) firmly packed
**   brown sugar**
½ cup (110g) castor sugar
3 eggs
2 cups (300g) plain flour
½ cup (50g) cocoa
1 teaspoon bicarbonate of soda
½ cup (125ml) sour cream
⅔ cup (160ml) water

Grease 23cm square slab cake pan, cover base with baking paper.

Combine all ingredients in medium bowl of electric mixer, beat on low speed until ingredients are combined. Then, beat on medium speed until mixture is just smooth and changed in colour; do not over-beat. Spread mixture into prepared pan. Bake in moderate oven about 50 minutes. Stand 5 minutes before turning onto wire rack to cool.

Top cold cake with 1 quantity Sour Cream Chocolate Glaze (page 121), if desired.

DATE AND HONEY LOAF

This cake is best made on day of serving.

185g butter, chopped
⅔ cup (160ml) honey
2 eggs
1½ cups (240g) wholemeal
**   self-raising flour**
½ cup (80g) wholemeal plain flour
½ cup (125ml) milk
½ cup (80g) chopped pitted dates

Grease 14cm x 21cm loaf pan, cover base with baking paper.

Combine butter, honey, eggs, flours, and milk in medium bowl of electric mixer, beat on low speed until ingredients are combined. Then, beat on medium speed until mixture is smooth and changed in colour. Stir in dates. Spread mixture into prepared pan. Bake in moderately slow oven about 1¼ hours. Turn onto wire rack to cool.

WHOLEMEAL HONEY BEER FRUIT CAKE

250g butter, chopped
1¼ cups (310ml) honey
3 eggs
1½ cups (240g) wholemeal
    self-raising flour
1½ cups (240g) wholemeal plain flour
1 teaspoon mixed spice
1½ cups (250g) chopped raisins
1½ cups (240g) chopped pitted dates
1½ cups (240g) sultanas
¾ cup (125g) mixed peel
¾ cup (110g) chopped dried apricots
⅓ cup (65g) chopped glace ginger
¼ cup (60g) glace cherries, quartered
375ml can beer

Line base and sides of deep 23cm square cake pan with 3 layers of baking paper, bringing paper 5cm above edges of pan.

Combine butter, honey, eggs, flours and spice in large bowl of electric mixer, beat on low speed until ingredients are combined. Then, beat on medium speed until mixture is smooth and changed in colour. Stir in fruit and beer. Spread into prepared pan. Bake in slow oven about 2¾ hours. Cover hot cake tightly with foil, cool in pan.

LEFT: Date and Honey Loaf.
BELOW LEFT: Chocolate Velvet Cake.
BELOW: Wholemeal Honey Beer Fruit Cake.

Left: Platter from Lyn Potter; cloth from Michael Feller Collections. Below left: China is Spode by Waterford Wedgwood. Below: China from Corso de Fiori; basket from In House Collections.

CHOCOLATE ALMOND CAKE

125g dark chocolate, melted
125g butter, chopped
1 cup (160g) icing sugar mixture
3 eggs
½ cup (75g) self-raising flour
¼ cup (60ml) milk
**1 cup (125g) packaged
    ground almonds**

Grease deep 18cm round cake pan, cover base with baking paper.

Combine chocolate, butter, icing sugar, eggs, flour and milk in medium bowl of electric mixer, beat on low speed until ingredients are combined. Then, beat on medium speed until mixture is smooth and changed in colour. Stir in nuts. Spread mixture into prepared pan. Bake in moderate oven about 1 hour. Stand few minutes before turning onto wire rack to cool.

Top cold cake with 1 quantity Chocolate Butter Cream (page 120), if desired.

CHOCOLATE CHIP PINEAPPLE CAKE

125g butter, chopped
1 teaspoon vanilla essence
¾ cup (165g) castor sugar
2 eggs
1⅓ cups (200g) self-raising flour
¼ cup (25g) cocoa
½ cup (125ml) milk
⅓ cup (65g) Choc Bits
**½ cup (115g) finely chopped
    glace pineapple**

Grease 20cm ring cake pan, cover base with baking paper.

Combine butter, essence, sugar, eggs, flour, cocoa and milk in medium bowl of electric mixer, beat on low speed until ingredients are combined. Then, beat on medium speed until mixture is smooth and changed in colour. Stir in remaining ingredients. Spoon mixture into prepared pan. Bake in moderate oven about 45 minutes. Stand cake few minutes before turning onto wire rack to cool.

Top cold cake with 1 quantity Chocolate Glace Icing (page 120) and extra chopped glace pineapple, if desired.

MARMALADE CAKE

125g butter, chopped
1 teaspoon grated orange rind
**¾ cup (150g) firmly packed
    brown sugar**
2 eggs
¼ cup (60ml) marmalade
1½ cups (225g) self-raising flour
¼ cup (60ml) milk

Grease 20cm ring cake pan. Combine all ingredients in medium bowl of electric mixer, beat on low speed until ingredients are combined. Then, beat on medium speed until mixture is smooth and changed in colour. Spread into prepared pan. Bake in moderate oven about 35 minutes. Turn onto wire rack to cool.

Top cold cake with 1 quantity Citrus Frosting (page 121) and mixed peel, if desired.

LEFT: From back: Chocolate Chip Pineapple Cake, Chocolate Almond Cake.
RIGHT: Marmalade Cake.

COCONUT FRUIT CAKE

185g butter, chopped
2 teaspoons coconut essence
½ cup (110g) castor sugar
3 eggs
1 cup (90g) coconut
½ cup (75g) plain flour
½ cup (75g) self-raising flour
½ cup (125ml) canned coconut milk
1 cup (190g) chopped dried figs
¾ cup (185g) chopped glace apricots
⅔ cup (110g) mixed peel
⅔ cup (110g) sultanas

Line base and side of deep 20cm round cake pan with 3 layers of baking paper, bringing paper 5cm above edge of pan.

Combine butter, essence, sugar, eggs, coconut, flours and coconut milk in medium bowl of electric mixer, beat on low speed until ingredients are combined. Then, beat on medium speed until mixture is changed in colour. Stir in fruit; mix well. Spread mixture into prepared pan. Bake in slow oven about 2 hours. Cover hot cake tightly with foil, cool in pan.

COCONUT BUTTER CAKE

125g butter, chopped
1 teaspoon coconut essence
1 cup (220g) castor sugar
4 eggs
½ cup (75g) self-raising flour
¼ cup (40g) semolina
1¼ cups (110g) coconut

Grease 15cm x 25cm loaf pan, line base and sides with baking paper.

Combine all ingredients in medium bowl of electric mixer, beat on low speed until ingredients are combined. Then, beat on medium speed until mixture is changed in colour. Spread mixture into prepared pan. Bake in moderate oven about 50 minutes. Turn onto wire rack to cool.

Top cold cake with 1 quantity Citrus Frosting (page 121) and flaked coconut, if desired.

PASSIONFRUIT BUTTER CAKE

You will need about 3 passionfruit for this cake.

125g butter, chopped
¾ cup (165g) castor sugar
2 eggs
2 cups (300g) self-raising flour
½ cup (125ml) milk
¼ cup passionfruit pulp

Grease 21cm baba cake pan. Combine butter, sugar, eggs, flour and milk in medium bowl of electric mixer, beat on low speed until ingredients are combined. Then, beat on medium speed until mixture is smooth and changed in colour. Stir in passionfruit. Spread into prepared pan. Bake in moderate oven about 45 minutes. Turn onto wire rack to cool.

Top cold cake with 1 quantity Passionfruit Glace Icing (page 120), if desired.

LEFT: From left: Coconut Butter Cake, Coconut Fruit Cake.
BELOW: Passionfruit Butter Cake.

Left: Platter and glass compote dish from Windsor Antique Market. Below: Plate, mugs and serviette from Accoutrement.

CARROT AND BANANA CAKE

You will need about 2 over-ripe medium bananas and about 200g carrots for this cake.

90g butter, chopped
1 cup (220g) raw sugar
1 egg
1½ cups (225g) plain flour
1 teaspoon bicarbonate of soda
¾ cup mashed banana
1 cup finely grated carrot,
   firmly packed
¾ cup (90g) walnut or pecan pieces

Grease 14cm x 21cm loaf pan, cover base with baking paper.

Combine butter, sugar, egg, flour, soda and banana in medium bowl of electric mixer, beat on low speed until ingredients are combined. Then, beat on medium speed until mixture is smooth and changed in colour. Stir in carrot and nuts. Spread mixture into prepared pan. Bake in moderate oven about 1¼ hours. Stand few minutes before turning onto wire rack to cool.

ORANGE TEA CAKE

150g butter, chopped
2 teaspoons grated orange rind
⅔ cup (150g) castor sugar
3 eggs
1 cup (150g) self-raising flour

Grease 20cm round sandwich cake pan, cover base with baking paper.

Combine all ingredients in small bowl of electric mixer, beat on low speed until ingredients are combined. Then, beat on medium speed until mixture is smooth and changed in colour. Spread into prepared pan. Bake in moderate oven about 40 minutes. Turn onto wire rack to cool.

Dust cold cake with sifted icing sugar, if desired.

LEFT: Carrot and Banana Cake.
ABOVE: From left: Orange Tea Cake, Orange Date Cake.

Left: Tray, basket, "apples" and serviette from Home & Garden on the Mall. Above: China from Corso de Fiori; serviette from Michael Feller Collections.

ORANGE DATE CAKE

125g butter, chopped
3 teaspoons grated orange rind
¾ cup (165g) castor sugar
2 eggs
⅓ cup (80ml) orange juice
1½ cups (225g) self-raising flour
¾ cup (120g) chopped pitted dates

Grease 20cm ring cake pan. Combine butter, rind, sugar, eggs, juice and flour in medium bowl of electric mixer, beat on low speed until ingredients are combined. Then, beat on medium speed until mixture is smooth and changed in colour. Stir in dates. Spoon mixture into prepared pan. Bake in moderate oven about 45 minutes. Turn onto wire rack to cool.

Top cold cake with 1 quantity Citrus Frosting (page 121) and fresh orange segments, if desired.

CHOCOLATE LOAF

125g dark chocolate, melted
125g butter, chopped
1 teaspoon vanilla essence
¾ cup (165g) castor sugar
2 eggs
1¾ cups (265g) self-raising flour
¾ cup (180ml) sour cream

Grease 14cm x 21cm loaf pan, cover base with baking paper.

Combine all ingredients in medium bowl of electric mixer, beat on low speed until ingredients are combined. Then, beat on medium speed until mixture is smooth and changed in colour. Spread mixture into prepared pan. Bake in moderate oven about 1 hour. Stand cake few minutes before turning onto wire rack to cool.

If desired, make 1½ quantities Chocolate Butter Cream (page 120), spread sides of cake with some of the butter cream, press on crushed nuts. Top cake with more butter cream and decorate with feather and fan design (page 123).

HONEY CHOCOLATE CAKE

90g dark chocolate, melted
125g butter, chopped
⅓ cup (75g) castor sugar
⅔ cup (160ml) honey
2 eggs
¾ cup (110g) plain flour
½ cup (75g) self-raising flour
¼ cup (60ml) water

Grease deep 19cm square cake pan, cover base with baking paper.

Combine all ingredients in medium bowl of electric mixer, beat on low speed until ingredients are combined. Then, beat on medium speed until mixture is smooth and changed in colour. Pour into prepared pan. Bake in moderate oven about 50 minutes. Stand few minutes before turning onto wire rack to cool.

Top cold cake with 1 quantity Honey Cream Cheese Frosting (page 121) marbled with ½ quantity Chocolate Butter Cream (page 120), if desired.

LIGHT LEMON CAKE

125g butter, chopped
2 teaspoons grated lemon rind
¾ cup (165g) castor sugar
2 eggs
1½ cups (225g) self-raising flour
2 tablespoons full cream milk powder
½ cup (125ml) water

Grease 20cm ring cake pan. Combine all ingredients in medium bowl of electric mixer, beat on low speed until ingredients are combined. Then, beat on medium speed until mixture is smooth and changed in colour. Pour into prepared pan. Bake in moderate oven about 40 minutes. Turn onto wire rack to cool.

Top cold cake with 1 quantity Citrus Frosting (page 121) and sprinkle with coconut, if desired.

LEFT: From left: Chocolate Loaf, Honey Chocolate Cake.
BELOW: Light Lemon Cake.

HONEYED GLACE FRUIT CAKE

250g butter, chopped
2 tablespoons honey
1 cup (220g) castor sugar
4 eggs
¼ cup (60ml) sweet sherry
1½ cups (225g) plain flour
¾ cup (110g) self-raising flour
½ cup (115g) finely chopped
glace pineapple
½ cup (125g) glace cherries, chopped
1 cup (200g) finely chopped
glace ginger
¼ cup (60g) finely chopped
glace apricots

Line base and sides of deep 19cm square cake pan with 3 layers of baking paper, bringing paper 5cm above edges of pan.

Combine butter, honey, sugar, eggs, sherry and flours in large bowl of electric mixer, beat on low speed until all ingredients are combined. Then, beat on medium speed until mixture is just smooth and changed in colour; do not over-beat. Stir in fruit. Spread mixture into prepared pan. Bake in slow oven about 2½ hours. Cover hot cake tightly with foil, cool in pan.

LIGHT WHOLEMEAL LEMON CAKE

250g butter, chopped
2 teaspoons grated lemon rind
1 cup (220g) castor sugar
4 eggs
¾ cup (120g) wholemeal
self-raising flour
¾ cup (110g) white plain flour

Grease deep 19cm square cake pan, cover base with baking paper.

Combine all ingredients in medium bowl of electric mixer, beat on low speed until ingredients are combined. Then, beat on medium speed until mixture is smooth and changed in colour. Spread into prepared pan. Bake in moderately slow oven about 1 hour. Stand 5 minutes before turning onto wire rack to cool.

Dust cold cake with sifted icing sugar, if desired.

LEFT: Light Wholemeal Lemon Cake.
BELOW: Honeyed Glace Fruit Cake.

Left: Serviette from Michael Feller Collections.

CITRUS BUTTER CAKE

125g butter, chopped
1 tablespoon grated orange rind
2 teaspoons grated lemon rind
¾ cup (165g) castor sugar
2 eggs
1½ cups (225g) self-raising flour
½ cup (125ml) milk

Grease 21cm baba cake pan. Combine all ingredients in medium bowl of electric mixer, beat on low speed until ingredients are combined. Then, beat on medium speed until mixture is smooth and changed in colour. Spread into prepared pan. Bake in moderate oven about 35 minutes. Turn onto wire rack to cool.

Drizzle cold cake with 1 quantity Orange Glace Icing (page 120) and top with orange shreds (page 123), if desired.

TRIPLE CHOC-ORANGE CAKE

125g butter, chopped
1 tablespoon grated orange rind
¾ cup (165g) castor sugar
2 eggs
1 cup (150g) self-raising flour
⅓ cup (50g) plain flour
2 tablespoons cocoa
100g dark chocolate, finely grated
⅓ cup (80ml) milk
⅔ cup (130g) Choc Bits

Grease 20cm ring cake pan, cover base with baking paper.

Combine butter, rind, sugar, eggs, flours, cocoa, chocolate and milk in medium bowl of electric mixer, beat on low speed until ingredients are combined. Then, beat on medium speed until mixture is smooth and changed in colour; stir in Choc Bits. Spoon and spread mixture into prepared pan. Bake in moderately slow oven about 1 hour. Stand 5 minutes before turning onto wire rack to cool.

Top cold cake with 1 quantity Citrus Frosting (page 121) and orange shreds (page 123), if desired.

CHOCOLATE FLECK CAKE

125g butter, chopped
½ cup (110g) castor sugar
3 eggs
60g dark chocolate, coarsely grated
1½ cups (225g) self-raising flour
¼ cup (60ml) milk

Grease 20cm ring cake pan. Combine all ingredients in medium bowl of electric mixer, beat on low speed until ingredients are combined. Then, beat on medium speed until mixture is smooth and changed in colour. Spread into prepared pan. Bake in moderate oven about 40 minutes. Turn onto wire rack to cool.

Top cold cake with 1 quantity Chocolate Glace Icing (page 120) and walnut halves, if desired.

BELOW: Citrus Butter Cake.
RIGHT: From left: Chocolate Fleck Cake, Triple Choc-Orange Cake.

Right: China from Limoges.

BANANA CARAMEL CAKE

You will need about 2 over-ripe medium bananas for this cake.

125g butter, chopped
1 cup (200g) firmly packed
   brown sugar
2 eggs
¾ cup mashed banana
1½ cups (225g) self-raising flour
¼ cup (60ml) milk

Grease 19cm x 29cm rectangular slice pan, cover base with baking paper.

Combine all ingredients in medium bowl of electric mixer, beat on low speed until ingredients are combined. Then, beat on medium speed until mixture is smooth and changed in colour. Spoon mixture into prepared pan. Bake in moderate oven about 40 minutes. Stand few minutes before turning onto wire rack to cool.

Top cold cake with 1 quantity Passion-fruit Cream Cheese Frosting (page 121), if desired.

ALMOND CARDAMOM CAKE

185g butter, chopped
¾ cup (150g) firmly packed
   brown sugar
⅓ cup (80ml) golden syrup
2 eggs
¼ cup (30g) packaged ground
   almonds
2 cups (300g) self-raising flour
2 teaspoons ground cardamom
½ cup (125ml) milk

Coat 21cm baba cake pan with non-stick spray. Combine all ingredients in medium bowl of electric mixer, beat on low speed until ingredients are combined. Then, beat on medium speed until mixture is smooth and changed in colour. Spread mixture into prepared pan. Bake in moderate oven about 55 minutes. Stand cake 5 minutes before turning onto wire rack to cool.

Drizzle cold cake with 1 quantity Lemon Glace Icing (page 120) and sprinkle with toasted flaked almonds (page 123), if desired.

SPICED CARAMEL CAKE

125g butter, chopped
1 cup (200g) firmly packed
   brown sugar
2 eggs
2 tablespoons golden syrup
1½ cups (225g) self-raising flour
1 teaspoon ground cinnamon
1 teaspoon ground nutmeg
½ teaspoon ground cloves
½ teaspoon ground ginger
½ cup (125ml) milk

Grease deep 20cm round cake pan, cover base and side with baking paper.

Combine all ingredients in medium bowl of electric mixer, beat on low speed until ingredients are combined. Then, beat on medium speed until mixture is just smooth and changed in colour; do not over-beat. Spoon mixture into prepared pan. Bake in moderate oven about 55 minutes. Stand 5 minutes before turning onto wire rack to cool.

Top cold cake with 1 quantity Citrus Frosting (page 121), if desired.

BELOW: Banana Caramel Cake.
RIGHT: From left: Spiced Caramel Cake, Almond Cardamom Cake.

Right: China from Royal Doulton.

VANILLA BUTTER CAKE

125g butter, chopped
2 teaspoons vanilla essence
¾ cup (165g) castor sugar
2 eggs
1 cup (150g) self-raising flour
1 tablespoon cornflour
¼ cup (60ml) milk

Coat 21cm baba cake pan with non-stick spray. Combine all ingredients in small bowl of electric mixer, beat on low speed until ingredients are combined. Then, beat on medium speed until mixture is smooth and changed in colour. Spoon mixture into prepared pan. Bake in moderate oven about 40 minutes. Stand few minutes before turning onto wire rack to cool.

Dust cold cake with sifted icing sugar, if desired.

COFFEE CARAMEL CAKE

125g butter, chopped
2 teaspoons vanilla essence
¾ cup (150g) firmly packed
   brown sugar
2 eggs
1 cup (150g) self-raising flour
¼ cup (30g) custard powder
3 teaspoons instant coffee powder
½ cup (125ml) milk

Grease 21cm baba cake pan. Combine all ingredients in medium bowl of electric mixer, beat on low speed until ingredients are combined. Then, beat on medium speed until mixture is smooth and changed in colour. Spread mixture into prepared pan. Bake in moderate oven about 40 minutes. Stand few minutes before turning onto wire rack to cool.

Top cold cake with 1 quantity Coffee Vienna Cream Frosting (page 121) and sprinkle with toasted flaked almonds (page 123), if desired.

HAZELNUT CHOCOLATE CAKE

125g butter, chopped
⅔ cup (150g) castor sugar
2 eggs
1½ cups (225g) self-raising flour
¼ cup (35g) plain flour
⅓ cup (80ml) hazelnut spread
⅔ cup (160ml) sour cream

Grease 14cm x 21cm loaf pan, cover base with baking paper.

Combine all ingredients in medium bowl of electric mixer, beat on low spead until ingredients are combined. Then, beat on medium speed until mixture is smooth and changed in colour. Spoon and spread mixture into prepared pan. Bake in moderate oven about 1 hour 10 minutes. Stand few minutes before turning onto wire rack to cool.

Top cold cake with 1 quantity Choc-Hazelnut Cream Cheese Frosting (page 121) and sprinkle with chopped hazelnuts, if desired.

RUM 'N' RAISIN COFFEE CAKE

185g butter, chopped
1/2 cup (110g) castor sugar
3 eggs
1½ cups (225g) self-raising flour
2 tablespoons milk
1 tablespoon dark rum
2 teaspoons instant coffee powder
1 cup (170g) chopped raisins

Grease deep 20cm round cake pan, cover base with baking paper.

Combine butter, sugar, eggs, flour, milk, rum and coffee in medium bowl of electric mixer, beat on low speed until ingredients are combined. Then, beat on medium speed until mixture is smooth and changed in colour. Stir in raisins. Spread mixture into prepared pan. Bake in moderate oven about 55 minutes. Stand 5 minutes before turning cake onto wire rack to cool.

Top cold cake with 1 quantity Coffee Vienna Cream Frosting (page 121), if desired.

LEFT: From back: Vanilla Butter Cake, Coffee Caramel Cake.
RIGHT: Rum 'n' Raisin Cake.
BELOW: Hazelnut Chocolate Cake.

Left: China from Royal Doulton.

CHERRY ORANGE CAKE

250g butter, chopped
1 tablespoon grated orange rind
1 cup (220g) castor sugar
4 eggs
½ cup (75g) self-raising flour
1½ cups (225g) plain flour
½ teaspoon bicarbonate of soda
½ cup (125ml) orange juice
½ cup (125g) chopped glace cherries

Grease deep 20cm round cake pan, cover base with baking paper.

Combine butter, rind, sugar, eggs, flours, soda and juice in medium bowl of electric mixer, beat on low speed until ingredients are combined. Then, beat on medium speed until mixture is smooth and changed in colour. Stir in cherries. Pour mixture into prepared pan. Bake in moderately slow oven about 1¼ hours. Stand 10 minutes before turning onto wire rack to cool.

CHERRY CHOCOLATE CAKE

125g butter, chopped
½ cup (100g) firmly packed brown sugar
2 eggs
½ cup (75g) plain flour
1 cup (150g) self-raising flour
½ teaspoon bicarbonate of soda
1 tablespoon cocoa
¼ cup (60ml) sour cream
½ cup (95g) Choc Bits
1 cup (210g) glace cherries, halved

Grease 14cm x 21cm loaf pan, cover base with baking paper.

Combine butter, sugar, eggs, flours, soda, cocoa and cream in medium bowl of electric mixer, beat on low speed until ingredients are combined. Then, beat on medium speed until mixture is smooth and changed in colour. Stir in Choc Bits and cherries. Spread mixture into prepared pan. Bake in moderately slow oven about 1½ hours. Stand 10 minutes before turning onto wire rack to cool.

Top cold cake with 1 quantity Chocolate Glace Icing (page 120) and decorate with extra glace cherries, if desired.

ZESTY LEMON CREAM CAKE

125g butter, chopped
1 tablespoon grated lemon rind
1 cup (220g) castor sugar
2 eggs
1½ cups (225g) self-raising flour
½ cup (125ml) sour cream

Grease 21cm baba cake pan. Combine all ingredients in medium bowl of electric mixer, beat on low speed until ingredients are combined. Then, beat on medium speed until mixture is smooth and changed in colour. Spoon and spread mixture into prepared pan. Bake in moderate oven about 50 minutes. Stand few minutes before turning onto wire rack to cool.

Dust cold cake with sifted icing sugar, if desired.

BELOW: From left: Cherry Orange Cake, Cherry Chocolate Cake.
RIGHT: Zesty Lemon Cream Cake.

Below: China from Royal Doulton; cherub, embroidered cushion and tassel from Home & Garden on the Mall.

Packet Mixes

Glamorous and lavishly decorated, these beauties are truly out of the box!
Half the preparation is already done, and it is simple to vary
different basic packet mixes.

OUR TIPS FOR SUCCESS

■ For best results in mixing, have all ingredients at room temperature, particularly butter.

■ Do not follow packet directions unless we tell you to do so. In some recipes, it is necessary to use the ingredients listed on the packet, but in other recipes we have changed or added ingredients. Follow directions carefully in our recipes.

CHOCOLATE ORANGE LIQUEUR CAKE

Use a cake mix that does not require butter to be added.

340g packet orange cake mix
60g butter, chopped
**¼ cup (30g) chopped
  roasted hazelnuts**
90g dark chocolate, melted
**2 tablespoons Grand Marnier
  or Cointreau**
**1 cup (125g) chopped roasted
  hazelnuts, extra**

FILLING
600ml thickened cream
2 tablespoons icing sugar mixture

Grease deep 23cm round cake pan, cover base with baking paper.

Place ingredients from sachet in small bowl, add butter and ingredients listed on packet. Follow method on packet for making cake. Fold in nuts and swirl in chocolate. Spread mixture into prepared pan. Bake in moderate oven about 50 minutes. Turn onto wire rack to cool.

Split cold cake in half horizontally. Sprinkle half the cake with half the liqueur, top with about quarter of the filling, top with remaining cake layer, sprinkle with remaining liqueur. Use remaining filling to decorate top and side of cake. Press extra nuts around side of cake. Decorate with extra whole nuts and orange shreds (page 123), if desired.

Filling: Beat cream and sugar in small bowl with electric mixer until firm.

RIGHT: Chocolate Orange Liqueur Cake.

China by Royal Worcester is available from Waterford Wedgwood.

CHOCOLATE CREAM CAKE

Use a cake mix that does not require butter to be added.

370g packet chocolate cake mix
60g butter, chopped
2 eggs
1/3 cup (80ml) water
1/2 cup (125ml) sour cream
60g dark chocolate, melted
100g dark chocolate, grated, extra
1 teaspoon icing sugar mixture
1 teaspoon cocoa

SYRUP
2 tablespoons castor sugar
2 tablespoons water
2 tablespoons Tia Maria or Kahlua

FILLING
185g unsalted butter, chopped
185g dark chocolate, melted

Grease deep 23cm round cake pan, cover base with baking paper.

Place ingredients from cake mix sachet in small bowl, add butter, eggs, water, sour cream and cooled melted chocolate (do not add ingredients listed on packet). Follow method on packet for making cake. Pour mixture into prepared pan. Bake in moderate oven about 50 minutes. Turn onto wire rack to cool.

Split cold cake horizontally into 3 layers, brush each layer with syrup. Sandwich layers together with one-third of filling. Cover top and side of cake with remaining filling. Decorate side with grated extra chocolate. Sprinkle cake with sifted icing sugar and cocoa, top with chocolate flakes (page 122), if desired.

Syrup: Combine sugar and water in small saucepan, stir over heat, without boiling, until sugar is dissolved; cool, stir in liqueur.

Filling: Beat butter in small bowl with electric mixer until light and fluffy. Gradually beat in cooled chocolate, beat well.

LEFT: Chocolate Cream Cake.
ABOVE: Berry Jelly Cake.

Left: China from Johnson Brothers; fork from Whitehill Silver and Plate Co. Pty Ltd; cushion and overcloth from Linen & Lace of Balmain.
Above: China from Villeroy & Boch.

BERRY JELLY CAKE

340g packet golden buttercake mix
85g packet raspberry jelly crystals
2/3 cup (160ml) milk
2 eggs
60g butter, chopped

Grease 15cm x 25cm loaf pan, cover base with baking paper.

Place ingredients from cake mix sachet (do not add ingredients listed on packet) and jelly crystals in small bowl, add milk, eggs and butter. Follow method on packet for making cake. Pour mixture into prepared pan. Bake in moderate oven about 50 minutes. Stand few minutes before turning onto wire rack to cool.

If desired, split cold cake into 3 layers, fill and decorate with 2 quantities Chantilly Cream (page 121) and strawberries. Press toasted flaked almonds (page 123) around sides of cake.

HONEY ROLL

280g packet golden sponge cake mix
2 eggs
1 teaspoon ground ginger
1 teaspoon ground cinnamon
½ teaspoon ground cloves
⅓ cup (80ml) water
2 tablespoons golden syrup
⅓ cup (30g) coconut

Grease 25cm x 35cm Swiss roll pan, cover base with baking paper.

Place ingredients from sachet in small bowl, add eggs, spices, water and golden syrup (do not add ingredients listed on packet). Follow method on packet for making cake. Spread mixture into prepared pan. Bake in moderate oven about 20 minutes or until lightly browned and elastic to touch.

Turn sponge onto sheet of greaseproof paper which has been sprinkled with coconut. Peel off baking paper, trim edges with sharp knife. Gently roll hot sponge from long side, rolling greaseproof paper inside; cool.

When sponge is cold, carefully unroll, spread with 1 quantity Chantilly Cream (page 121), reroll carefully.

CHOCOLATE PUDDING CAKE

Use a cake mix that does not require butter to be added.

370g packet chocolate cake mix
85g packet chocolate instant pudding dessert mix
¼ cup (60ml) vegetable oil
60g unsalted butter, chopped
3 eggs
¾ cup (180ml) water

Grease 21cm baba cake pan. Place ingredients from both sachets into small bowl with oil, butter, eggs and water (do not add ingredients listed on packets). Follow method for mixing on cake mix packet. Pour mixture into prepared pan. Bake in moderate oven about 50 minutes. Stand few minutes before turning onto wire rack to cool.

Top cold cake with 1 quantity Chocolate Cream Topping (page 121), refrigerate cake to set topping. Decorate with chocolate curls (page 122) and sifted icing sugar, if desired.

BELOW: Honey Roll.
RIGHT: Chocolate Pudding Cake.

Below: China from Royal Doulton; rug from Parker's of Turramurra. Right: China from Royal Doulton; cake server and forks from Cottage Manner.

BANANA CINNAMON CAKE

You will need about 2 medium over-ripe bananas and 1 firm medium banana for this cake.

340g packet golden buttercake mix
1 teaspoon ground cinnamon
⅔ cup mashed over-ripe banana
1 firm banana, finely chopped

Grease 23cm square slab cake pan, cover base with baking paper.

Place ingredients from cake mix sachet in small bowl, add cinnamon, mashed banana and ingredients listed on packet. Follow method on packet for making cake. Fold in chopped banana. Pour mixture into prepared pan. Bake in moderate oven about 40 minutes. Turn onto wire rack to cool.

Top cold cake with 1 quantity Cinnamon Vienna Cream Frosting (page 121), and decorate with extra banana slices dipped in lemon juice, if desired.

RIGHT: Banana Cinnamon Cake.

Right: China by Royal Worcester is available from Waterford Wedgwood; serviette from Linen & Lace of Balmain.

Saucepan Method

You can mix an amazing variety of cakes in a saucepan, without any bowls or mess. The cakes have moist textures, and fruit is plump and succulent. There's even a sweet bonus — lots less washing-up!

OUR TIPS FOR SUCCESS

- Read methods of recipes carefully and do not boil mixtures unless specified; evaporation of liquid is to be avoided.
- Use a medium-sized saucepan for most of these cakes; we have specified when to use a large saucepan, mainly for fruit cakes.
- We like to use a wooden spoon for mixing.
- Cool or stand mixtures for the time specified in recipes.
- Sometimes ingredients are added to a hot mixture; it's essential to stir quickly.
- The melting or boiling processes which are done in the saucepan can be done in a microwave oven, using a microwave ovenproof bowl, if preferred.
- See page 123 for instructions on how to line your cake pans.

BOILED PASSIONFRUIT FRUIT CAKE

You will need about 12 medium passionfruit (1 cup/250ml passionfruit pulp) for this cake.

½ cup (125ml) strained
    passionfruit juice
125g butter, chopped
2¾ cups (500g) mixed dried fruit
¼ cup (60ml) orange juice
1 cup (220g) sugar
3 eggs
¾ cup (110g) plain flour
¾ cup (110g) self-raising flour

Line base and side of deep 20cm round cake pan with 3 layers of baking paper, bringing paper 5cm above edge of pan.

Place passionfruit juice, butter, fruit, orange juice and sugar in large saucepan, bring to boil, stirring, then simmer, uncovered, 3 minutes; cover, cool.

Stir eggs and flours into fruit mixture, pour into prepared pan. Bake in moderately slow oven about 1½ hours. Cover hot cake tightly with foil, cool in pan.

Dust cold cake with sifted icing sugar, if desired.

RIGHT: Boiled Passionfruit Fruit Cake.

Cake slice from Country Road Homewear.

MELT 'N' MIX COFFEE CAKE

125g butter, chopped
2/3 cup (130g) firmly packed brown sugar
1/3 cup (75g) castor sugar
1/2 cup (125ml) milk
2 teaspoons instant coffee powder
2 eggs
1 1/2 cups (225g) self-raising flour

Grease 14cm x 21cm loaf pan, cover base with baking paper.

Combine butter, sugars, milk and coffee powder in medium saucepan, stir over low heat, without boiling, until butter is melted. Stand 10 minutes.

Stir in eggs and flour. Pour into prepared pan. Bake in moderate oven about 40 minutes. Turn onto wire rack to cool.

Top cold cake with 1 quantity Coffee Glace Icing (page 120) and decorate with walnuts, if desired.

QUICK 'N' EASY BUTTER CAKE

125g butter, chopped
3/4 cup (180ml) milk
1 cup (220g) castor sugar
3 eggs
2 teaspoons vanilla essence
1 1/2 cups (225g) self-raising flour

Grease 20cm ring cake pan, line base and side with baking paper.

Place butter, milk and sugar in medium saucepan, stir over heat, without boiling, until sugar is dissolved and butter melted; cool 10 minutes.

Stir in eggs, essence and flour. Pour into prepared pan. Bake in moderate oven about 45 minutes. Stand 5 minutes before turning onto wire rack to cool.

Dust cold cake with a little sifted icing sugar, if desired.

SWEET ORANGE LOAF

90g butter, chopped
3/4 cup (165g) castor sugar
3/4 cup (180ml) milk
1 tablespoon grated orange rind
1 egg
1 1/2 cups (225g) self-raising flour

Grease 14cm x 21cm loaf pan, cover base with baking paper.

Combine butter, sugar, milk and rind in

MELT 'N' MIX CHOC-GINGER CAKE

90g butter, chopped
2/3 cup (160ml) golden syrup
1/2 cup (110g) castor sugar
1/2 cup (125ml) milk
2 eggs
1 cup (150g) plain flour
1/2 cup (75g) self-raising flour
1/4 cup (25g) cocoa
3 teaspoons ground ginger
1/2 teaspoon bicarbonate of soda

Grease 20cm ring cake pan, cover base with baking paper.

Place butter, golden syrup and sugar in medium saucepan, stir over low heat, without boiling, until butter is melted; cool 5 minutes. Stir in milk, eggs and dry ingredients, stir until smooth. Pour mixture into prepared pan. Bake in moderate oven about 40 minutes. Stand 5 minutes before turning onto wire rack to cool.

Top cold cake with 1 quantity Chocolate Fudge Frosting (page 121), and sprinkle with slivered almond kernels, if desired.

medium saucepan, stir over low heat, without boiling, until butter is melted; cool 10 minutes. Stir in egg and flour. Pour mixture into prepared pan. Bake in moderate oven about 40 minutes. Turn onto wire rack to cool.

Top cold cake with 1 quantity Orange Vienna Cream Frosting (page 121) and sprinkle with mixed peel, if desired.

ABOVE: Clockwise from top: Sweet Orange Loaf, Quick 'n' Easy Butter Cake, Melt 'n' Mix Coffee Cake.
RIGHT: Melt 'n' Mix Choc-Ginger Cake.

Above: China from On Broadway Antique Market.
Right: China from Waterford Wedgwood, tray from Parker's of Turramurra.

WHOLEMEAL APRICOT ROLLS

1 cup (150g) chopped dried apricots
1 cup (250ml) water
1 teaspoon bicarbonate of soda
90g butter, chopped
¾ cup (150g) firmly packed
**   brown sugar**
1 egg
1¼ cups (185g) white plain flour
1 cup (160g) wholemeal
**   self-raising flour**
⅓ cup (30g) coconut

Grease 2 nut roll tins (8cm x 17cm). Place apricots and water in medium saucepan, bring to boil, remove from heat, stir in soda and butter; cool 10 minutes. Stir remaining ingredients into apricot mixture. Spoon into tins, cover with lids, place tins upright on oven tray. Bake in moderate oven about 1 hour. Stand 5 minutes before removing from tins, cool on wire racks.

EGGLESS DATE AND NUT ROLLS

1 cup (160g) chopped pitted dates
1 cup (250ml) water
1 cup (220g) castor sugar
60g butter, chopped
1 cup (150g) plain flour
1 cup (150g) self-raising flour
1 teaspoon bicarbonate of soda
½ cup (60g) chopped walnuts

Grease 2 nut roll tins (8cm x 17cm). Place dates, water, sugar and butter in medium saucepan, stir over heat, without boiling, until sugar is dissolved. Bring to boil, simmer, covered, 4 minutes; cool 10 minutes. Stir flours, soda and nuts into date mixture. Spoon mixture into prepared tins, cover with lids, place tins upright on oven tray. Bake in moderate oven about 1 hour. Stand 5 minutes before removing from tins, cool on wire racks.

NUT ROLL TINS

If nut roll tins are unavailable, cans which have contained fruit juice can be substituted. Wash and grease cans well. Only half fill cans with mixture, cover open ends tightly with foil; bake as directed in recipes.

ABOVE: From left on bread board: Wholemeal Apricot Rolls, Eggless Date and Nut Rolls.
RIGHT: From left: Melt 'n' Mix Fruit Cake, Old-Fashioned Boiled Fruit Cake.

Above: China from Villeroy & Boch; rug from Linen & Lace of Balmain. Right: China from Royal Doulton; lacy overcloth from Linen & Lace of Balmain; fabric from Les Olivades.

MELT 'N' MIX FRUIT CAKE

250g butter, chopped
1/2 cup (125ml) milk
2 cups (400g) firmly packed
   brown sugar
1kg (5 cups) mixed dried fruit
2 tablespoons sweet sherry
1 teaspoon mixed spice
3 cups (450g) plain flour
1/2 teaspoon bicarbonate of soda
3 eggs
1/2 teaspoon almond essence
1/2 teaspoon lemon essence

Line base and side of deep 23cm round cake pan with 3 layers of baking paper, bringing paper 5cm above edge of pan.

Place butter, milk and sugar in large saucepan, stir over heat, without boiling, until butter is melted. Stir in remaining ingredients. Spread mixture into prepared pan. Decorate with blanched almonds, if desired. Bake in slow oven about 3 hours. Cover hot cake tightly with foil, cool in pan.

OLD-FASHIONED BOILED FRUIT CAKE

125g butter, chopped
1 cup (220g) sugar
1 cup (250ml) water
1 tablespoon golden syrup
1 teaspoon mixed spice
4 cups (750g) mixed dried fruit
2 eggs
1 cup (150g) plain flour
1 cup (150g) self-raising flour

Line base and side of deep 20cm round cake pan with 3 layers of baking paper, bringing paper 5cm above edge of pan.

Place butter, sugar, water, golden syrup, spice and fruit in large saucepan. Bring to boil, stirring, then simmer, uncovered, 3 minutes; cover, cool.

Stir in eggs and flours. Spoon mixture into prepared pan. Bake in moderately slow oven about 2 hours. Cover hot cake tightly with foil, cool in pan.

HONEY WALNUT WHOLEMEAL LOAF

185g butter, chopped
⅓ cup (80ml) milk
2 tablespoons honey
⅓ cup (65g) brown sugar
½ teaspoon bicarbonate of soda
¾ cup (110g) white plain flour
½ cup (80g) wholemeal
   self-raising flour
½ cup (60g) chopped walnuts
1 egg

Grease 14cm x 21cm loaf pan, cover base with baking paper.

Place butter, milk, honey and sugar in medium saucepan, stir over low heat, without boiling, until butter is melted. Stand 10 minutes. Stir in soda, flours, nuts and egg. Pour mixture into prepared pan. Bake in moderate oven about 40 minutes. Stand 5 minutes before turning onto wire rack to cool.

Top cold cake with 1 quantity Honey Cream Cheese Frosting (page 121), if desired.

LEFT: Honey Walnut Wholemeal Loaf.
RIGHT: From left: Rich Brandied Date Cake, Boiled Date Cake.
BELOW: Condensed Milk Fruit Cake.

Left: Jug from On Broadway Antique Market; egg basket from Made on Earth.
Right: Candles from Made on Earth.
Below: Tins from In House Collections.

CONDENSED MILK FRUIT CAKE

4 cups (750g) mixed dried fruit
1/2 cup (125ml) water
1 cup (150g) self-raising flour
1 egg
400g can sweetened condensed milk

Line base and side of deep 20cm round cake pan with 3 layers of baking paper, bringing paper 5cm above edge of pan.

Place fruit and water in large saucepan, bring to boil, simmer, uncovered, 1 minute; cover, cool to room temperature.

Stir remaining ingredients into fruit mixture, spoon into prepared pan. Bake in slow oven about 2 hours. Cover hot cake tightly with foil, cool in pan.

BOILED DATE CAKE

185g butter, chopped
1 cup (170g) pitted dates,
   finely chopped
1/2 cup (100g) firmly packed
   brown sugar
1 cup (250ml) milk
1/2 teaspoon bicarbonate of soda
2 eggs
2 1/4 cups (335g) self-raising flour

Grease deep 20cm round cake pan, cover base with baking paper.

Place butter, dates, sugar and milk in medium saucepan, bring to boil, remove from heat. Stir in soda, stand 10 minutes. Stir in eggs and flour. Spoon mixture into prepared pan. Bake in moderate oven about 50 minutes. Stand 10 minutes before turning onto wire rack to cool.

RICH BRANDIED DATE CAKE

3 cups (500g) chopped pitted dates
1 cup (250ml) water
2 cup-size tea bags
1 teaspoon bicarbonate of soda
300g butter, chopped
1 1/2 cups (330g) castor sugar
4 eggs
2 1/2 cups (250g) walnuts
1 cup (150g) plain flour
1/2 cup (75g) self-raising flour
1/3 cup (80ml) brandy

Grease deep 23cm round cake pan, line base and side with baking paper.

Combine dates and water in medium saucepan, bring to boil, remove from heat. Add tea bags and soda, cover, stand 15 minutes. Discard tea bags, add butter and sugar to pan, stir until butter is melted. Stir in eggs, nuts, flours and brandy. Pour mixture into prepared pan. Bake in slow oven about 2 hours. Cool in pan.

CHERRY COCONUT CAKE

150g butter
1½ cups (135g) coconut
1½ cups (225g) self-raising flour
1 cup (220g) castor sugar
3 eggs
¾ cup (180ml) milk
½ cup (125g) finely chopped red
  glace cherries

Grease deep 20cm round cake pan, line base and side with baking paper.

Melt butter in medium saucepan. Stir in remaining ingredients. Pour mixture into prepared pan. Bake in moderate oven about 1 hour. Stand cake few minutes before turning onto wire rack to cool.

Top cold cake with 2 quantities Chocolate Butter Cream (page 120); decorate with flaked coconut and maraschino cherries, if desired.

ORANGE RAISIN BREAD

1½ cups (250g) raisins, chopped
30g butter
1 cup (220g) castor sugar
1½ cups (375ml) water
2 teaspoons grated orange rind
¼ cup (60ml) orange juice
1 egg
2½ cups (375g) self-raising flour

Grease 2 x 8cm x 26cm bar cake pans, cover bases with baking paper.

Place raisins, butter, sugar and water in medium saucepan. Bring to boil, stirring, then simmer, uncovered, 2 minutes. Remove from heat, stir in rind and juice; cool. Stir egg and flour into raisin mixture. Spread mixture into prepared pans. Bake in moderate oven about 40 minutes. Turn onto wire rack to cool.

CHEESE 'N' RAISIN NUT BREAD

1½ cups (250g) chopped raisins
1 cup (250ml) water
½ cup (110g) sugar
1¾ cups (260g) self-raising flour
1 cup (125g) grated tasty cheese
½ cup (60g) chopped pecans
**   or walnuts**
1 egg

Grease 14cm x 21cm loaf pan, cover base with baking paper.

Combine raisins and water in medium saucepan, bring to boil, remove from heat; cover, stand 15 minutes. Stir in remaining ingredients. Spoon mixture into prepared pan. Bake in moderately slow oven about 1 hour. Stand 5 minutes before turning onto wire rack to cool.

FRUIT AND NUT BREAD

½ cup (80g) chopped pitted dates
½ cup (75g) chopped dried apricots
½ cup (75g) unsalted roasted
**   cashews**
125g butter, chopped
⅔ cup (150g) raw sugar
¾ cup (180ml) water
½ teaspoon bicarbonate of soda
¼ cup (20g) coconut
2 tablespoons brandy
2 eggs
¾ cup (120g) wholemeal
**   self-raising flour**
¾ cup (120g) wholemeal plain flour

Grease 14cm x 21cm loaf pan, cover base with baking paper.

Place fruit, nuts, butter, sugar and water in medium saucepan. Bring to boil, stirring; remove from heat. Stir in soda, coconut and brandy, cover, cool 1 hour.

Stir eggs and flours into fruit mixture. Spoon into prepared pan. Bake in moderate oven about 1 hour. Turn onto wire rack to cool.

LEFT: Cherry Coconut Cake.
BELOW: From left: Fruit and Nut Bread, Cheese 'n' Raisin Nut Bread, Orange Raisin Bread.

Left: Embroidered cushion and tassel from Linen & Lace of Balmain; platter from Whitehill Silver and Plate Co. Pty Ltd.

CARROT RAISIN BREAD

You will need about 200g carrots for this loaf.

1 cup (170g) raisins, chopped
1 cup coarsely grated carrot
¾ cup (180ml) water
¾ cup (165g) sugar
30g butter
1 teaspoon ground cinnamon
¾ cup (110g) self-raising flour
¾ cup (110g) plain flour
½ teaspoon bicarbonate of soda
½ cup (60g) chopped walnuts

Grease 14cm x 21cm loaf pan, cover base with paper.

Place raisins, carrot, water, sugar, butter and cinnamon in medium saucepan. Stir over heat, without boiling, until sugar is dissolved, then simmer, covered, 10 minutes; cool to room temperature. Stir in remaining ingredients. Spread mixture into prepared pan. Bake in moderately slow oven about 1 hour. Stand few minutes before turning onto wire rack to cool.

CARROT, CARAWAY AND HONEY LOAF

You will need about 500g carrots for this loaf.

250g butter, chopped
¾ cup (150g) firmly packed brown sugar
½ cup (125ml) honey
4 eggs
3 cups coarsely grated carrot
2 cups (320g) wholemeal plain flour
1 teaspoon bicarbonate of soda
3 teaspoons caraway seeds

Grease 15cm x 25cm loaf pan, cover base with paper.

Place butter, sugar and honey in medium saucepan, stir over heat, without boiling, until sugar is dissolved; cool to room temperature. Stir in eggs, carrot, flour, soda and seeds. Pour into prepared pan. Bake in moderately slow oven about 1¼ hours. Stand 5 minutes before turning onto wire rack to cool.

Top cold cake with 1 quantity Honey Cream Cheese Frosting (page 121) and sprinkle with extra caraway seeds, if desired.

BELOW: From left: Carrot Raisin Bread, Carrot, Caraway and Honey Loaf.

Bread board and canisters from Country Furniture Antiques; serviette from Linen & Lace of Balmain.

BOILED APRICOT NECTAR CAKE

1²⁄₃ cups (250g) chopped
   dried apricots
½ cup (125ml) apricot nectar
½ cup (110g) castor sugar
½ cup (100g) firmly packed
   brown sugar
250g butter, chopped
3 eggs
1 cup (150g) plain flour
1 cup (150g) self-raising flour

Grease 15cm x 25cm loaf pan, line base and sides with 1 layer of baking paper; bringing paper 5cm above edges of pan.

Place apricots, nectar and sugars in medium saucepan. Bring to boil, stirring, then simmer, covered, 5 minutes. Remove from heat, add butter, stir until melted; cover, cool to room temperature.

Stir eggs and flours into apricot mixture, spoon into prepared pan. Bake in slow oven about 1½ hours. Cover hot cake tightly with foil, cool in pan.

WHOLEMEAL APRICOT CAKE

125g butter, chopped
1¼ cups (185g) chopped
   dried apricots
2 teaspoons grated orange rind
2 tablespoons honey
²⁄₃ cup (160ml) milk
½ cup (110g) raw sugar
1 cup (160g) wholemeal
   self-raising flour
1 cup (150g) white self-raising flour
1 egg

Grease 14cm x 21cm loaf pan, cover base with paper.

Place butter, apricots, rind, honey, milk and sugar in medium saucepan. Bring to boil, stirring, remove from heat; cover, cool 1 hour.

Stir remaining ingredients into apricot mixture. Spread into prepared pan. Bake in moderate oven about 55 minutes. Turn onto wire rack to cool.

ABOVE: From left: Wholemeal Apricot Cake, Boiled Apricot Nectar Cake.

Canisters from On Broadway Antique Market.

MOIST DATE CAKE

3 cups (500g) chopped pitted dates
185g butter, chopped
⅔ cup (150g) castor sugar
1 cup (250ml) water
1 teaspoon bicarbonate of soda
3 eggs
1 cup (150g) self-raising flour
½ cup (75g) plain flour

Grease deep 19cm square cake pan, cover base with baking paper.

Place dates, butter, sugar, water and soda in medium saucepan. Bring to boil, stirring, remove from heat; cover, cool 30 minutes.

Stir eggs and flours into date mixture; mix well. Spoon mixture into prepared pan. Bake in moderately slow oven about 1¼ hours. Stand cake 10 minutes before turning onto wire rack to cool.

CHOCOLATE WALNUT BROWNIES

220g dark chocolate, chopped
150g butter, chopped
¼ cup (60ml) water
¾ cup (165g) castor sugar
1 cup (150g) self-raising flour
3 eggs
150g dark chocolate, chopped, extra
¾ cup (90g) chopped walnuts

Grease 23cm square slab cake pan, line with strip of baking paper to cover base and extend over 2 opposite sides of pan for easy lifting when cooked.

Place chocolate, butter, water and sugar in medium saucepan, stir over low heat, without boiling, until chocolate is melted; cool 10 minutes. Stir in flour, eggs, extra chocolate and nuts. Pour mixture into prepared pan. Bake in moderately slow oven about 45 minutes. Cool in pan.

Dust with combined equal quantities of sifted icing sugar and cocoa, if desired.

EGGLESS GINGER JUMBLE CAKE

185g butter, chopped
¾ cup (180ml) golden syrup
¾ cup (180ml) water
½ cup (100g) firmly packed
   brown sugar
2¼ cups (335g) plain flour
1½ teaspoons bicarbonate of soda
1½ tablespoons ground ginger
1½ teaspoons mixed spice
¼ teaspoon ground cloves

Grease 23cm square slab cake pan, cover base with paper.

Place butter, golden syrup, water and sugar in medium saucepan, stir over heat, without boiling, until butter is melted; cool 10 minutes. Stir in flour, soda and spices. Pour mixture into prepared pan. Bake in moderate oven about 40 minutes. Stand 5 minutes before turning onto wire rack to cool.

Top cold cake with 1 quantity pink and white marbled Cream Cheese Frosting (page 121), if desired.

LEFT: Moist Date Cake.
RIGHT: Eggless Ginger Jumble Cake.
BELOW: Chocolate Walnut Brownies.

Left: China from Royal Doulton; spread and white jug from Parker's of Turramurra. Right: Fabric from Les Olivades.

GOLDEN SYRUP COCONUT CAKE

125g butter, chopped
½ cup (125ml) golden syrup
2 cups (300g) self-raising flour
¼ cup (55g) castor sugar
½ cup (35g) shredded coconut
2 eggs
1 cup (250ml) milk

Grease 21cm baba cake pan. Combine butter and golden syrup in medium saucepan, stir over low heat until butter is melted; do not boil. Remove from heat, stir in remaining ingredients. Pour mixture into prepared pan. Bake in moderate oven about 40 minutes. Stand few minutes before turning onto wire rack to cool.

Drizzle cold cake with 1 quantity Lemon Glace Icing (page 120) and sprinkle with extra toasted shredded coconut (page 122), if desired.

BOILED CHOCOLATE CAKE

185g butter, chopped
1¼ cups (275g) sugar
⅓ cup (35g) cocoa
½ teaspoon bicarbonate of soda
⅓ cup (80ml) water
¾ cup (180ml) milk
2 eggs
2¼ cups (335g) self-raising flour

Grease 23cm square slab cake pan, cover base with baking paper.

Place butter, sugar, cocoa, soda, water and milk in medium saucepan, stir over heat until butter is melted. Bring to boil; cool to room temperature.

Add eggs and flour to mixture, stir until smooth. Pour mixture into prepared pan. Bake in moderate oven about 40 minutes. Stand few minutes before turning onto wire rack to cool.

Top cold cake with 1 quantity Rich Chocolate Glace Icing (page 120), if desired.

MOIST DOUBLE CHOCOLATE CAKE

125g butter, chopped
¾ cup (180ml) water
2 tablespoons cocoa
100g dark chocolate, chopped
1 cup (220g) sugar
¾ cup (110g) self-raising flour
½ cup (75g) plain flour
1 egg

Grease deep 20cm round cake pan, line base and side with baking paper.

Place butter, water, cocoa, chocolate and sugar in medium saucepan, stir over heat, without boiling, until sugar is dissolved; cool to room temperature.

Stir flours and egg into mixture, pour into prepared pan. Bake in moderately slow oven about 1 hour. Stand 5 minutes before turning onto wire rack to cool.

If desired, split cold cake, fill and top with 2 quantities Chantilly Cream (page 121) and sprinkle with chocolate shavings, (page 122).

LEFT: Golden Syrup Coconut Cake.
BELOW: From left: Boiled Chocolate Cake, Moist Double Chocolate Cake.

Below: China from Villeroy & Boch; wooden tray from Accoutrement.

CHOCOLATE DATE DESSERT CAKE

1 cup (160g) chopped pitted dates
250g butter, chopped
1¾ cups (430ml) water
1 cup (220g) sugar
⅓ cup (35g) cocoa
1⅔ cups (250g) plain flour
1 teaspoon bicarbonate of soda

Grease 19cm x 29cm rectangular slice pan, cover base with baking paper.

Combine dates, butter, water, sugar and cocoa in medium saucepan. Bring to boil, stirring, then simmer, uncovered, 5 minutes; cover, cool to room temperature.

Stir flour and soda into mixture, pour mixture into prepared pan. Bake in moderate oven about 40 minutes. Stand 5 minutes before turning onto wire rack to cool.

Serve cake warm or cold with whipped cream and chocolate shavings (page 122), if desired.

BELOW: *Chocolate Date Dessert Cake.*
RIGHT: *Clockwise from back: Date and Bran Loaf, Malted Date Loaf, Date and Coconut Cake.*

Right: Egg holder from Morris Home & Garden Wares.

DATE AND COCONUT CAKE

1½ cups (240g) chopped pitted dates
125g butter, chopped
1 cup (250ml) water
½ teaspoon bicarbonate of soda
¾ cup (150g) firmly packed
   brown sugar
2 eggs
1 cup (150g) plain flour
¾ cup (110g) self-raising flour
½ cup (45g) coconut

Grease 15cm x 25cm loaf pan, cover base with baking paper.

Place dates, butter, water, soda and sugar into medium saucepan. Bring to boil, stirring, then simmer, uncovered, 2 minutes; cover, cool to room temperature.

Stir eggs, flours and coconut into mixture, then spoon into prepared pan. Bake in moderate oven about 1 hour. Turn onto wire rack to cool.

DATE AND BRAN LOAF

125g butter, chopped
½ cup (125ml) golden syrup
1 cup (250ml) milk
1 cup (160g) chopped pitted dates
3 cups (450g) self-raising flour
½ cup (40g) unprocessed bran
1 teaspoon mixed spice
1 egg

Grease 14cm x 21cm loaf pan, cover base with baking paper.

Combine butter, golden syrup and milk in medium saucepan, stir over heat, without boiling, until butter is melted (mixture might appear curdled, but proceed); cover, cool.

Stir dates, flour, bran, spice and egg into mixture, spread into prepared pan. Bake in moderately slow oven about 1 hour 10 minutes. Stand 5 minutes before turning onto wire rack to cool.

MALTED DATE LOAF

30g butter
2 tablespoons malt extract
2 tablespoons golden syrup
¾ cup (180ml) milk
1 egg
1½ cups (225g) self-raising flour
2 tablespoons wheatgerm
¾ cup (120g) chopped pitted dates

Grease 14cm x 21cm loaf pan, cover base with baking paper.

Place butter, malt and golden syrup in medium saucepan, stir over heat, without boiling, until butter is melted; cool 5 minutes. Stir in milk, egg, flour, wheatgerm and dates. Spread mixture into prepared pan. Bake in moderately slow oven about 1 hour. Turn onto wire rack to cool.

TREACLE GINGER LOAF

90g butter, chopped
½ cup (125ml) milk
½ cup (125ml) treacle
1 egg
½ cup (110g) castor sugar
3 teaspoons ground ginger
1 cup (150g) self-raising flour
1 cup (150g) plain flour

Grease 15cm x 25cm loaf pan, cover base with baking paper.

Place butter, milk and treacle in medium saucepan, stir over heat, without boiling, until butter is melted. Stand 10 minutes. Stir in egg, sugar, ginger and flours. Spread into prepared pan. Bake in moderately slow oven about 1 hour. Stand few minutes before turning onto wire rack to cool.

Top cold cake with 1 quantity Treacle Cream Cheese Frosting (page 121), if desired.

SPICY BUTTERMILK GINGERBREAD

250g butter, chopped
1 cup (220g) sugar
1 cup (250ml) golden syrup
2 eggs
1 cup (250ml) buttermilk
1 teaspoon bicarbonate of soda
3 cups (450g) plain flour
1 teaspoon ground ginger
1 teaspoon ground cinnamon
1 teaspoon ground nutmeg
1 teaspoon mixed spice
¼ teaspoon ground cloves

Grease 23cm square slab cake pan, cover base with baking paper.

Place butter, sugar and golden syrup in medium saucepan, stir over heat, without boiling, until butter is melted. Stir in eggs, buttermilk, soda, flour and spices. Pour mixture into prepared pan. Bake in moderately slow oven about 1 hour. Stand cake 5 minutes before turning onto wire rack to cool.

Top cold cake with 1 quantity Citrus Frosting (page 121), if desired.

RIGHT: From back: Treacle Ginger Loaf, Spicy Buttermilk Gingerbread.
FAR RIGHT: From left: Wholemeal Boiled Sultana Cake, Sultana Marmalade Loaf.

Right: Fabric from I. Redelman & Son Pty. Ltd.
Far right: China and canisters from Country Furniture Antiques.

WHOLEMEAL BOILED SULTANA CAKE

4½ cups (750g) sultanas
1¾ cups (430ml) water
1 cup (200g) firmly packed
 brown sugar
1 tablespoon grated orange rind
½ cup (125ml) orange juice
½ cup (125ml) vegetable oil
3 eggs
1 cup (100g) soya flour
1¾ cups (280g) wholemeal
 self-raising flour

Line base and sides of greased deep 19cm square cake pan with baking paper.

Place sultanas, water and sugar in large saucepan, bring to boil, stirring, then simmer, uncovered, 3 minutes. Stir in rind, juice and oil, cool to room temperature.

Stir in eggs and flours. Pour mixture into prepared pan. Bake in moderately slow oven about 1¾ hours. Cover hot cake tightly with foil, cool in pan.

SULTANA MARMALADE LOAF

125g butter, chopped
3 cups (500g) sultanas
½ cup (100g) firmly packed
 brown sugar
2 tablespoons marmalade
¼ cup (60ml) sweet sherry
2 eggs
¾ cup (110g) plain flour
¼ cup (35g) self-raising flour

Line base and sides of 14cm x 21cm loaf pan with 3 layers of baking paper, bringing paper 5cm above edges of pan.

Place butter, sultanas, sugar, marmalade and sherry in medium saucepan, stir over heat, without boiling, until sugar is dissolved; cover, cool.

Stir eggs and flours into mixture, pour into prepared pan. Bake in slow oven about 1½ hours. Cover hot cake tightly with foil, cool in pan.

BOILED PINEAPPLE FRUIT CAKE

125g butter, chopped
450g can crushed pineapple
  in heavy syrup
2 cups (375g) mixed dried fruit
1 cup (220g) sugar
1 teaspoon mixed spice
1 teaspoon bicarbonate of soda
1 cup (150g) self-raising flour
1 cup (150g) plain flour
2 eggs

Grease 23cm square slab cake pan, line base and sides with baking paper.

Place butter, undrained pineapple, fruit, sugar and spice in medium saucepan. Bring to boil, stirring, then simmer, uncovered, 10 minutes. Stir in soda; cover, cool to room temperature.

Stir flours and eggs into mixture, spread mixture into prepared pan. Bake in moderately slow oven about 1 hour 10 minutes. Cover hot cake tightly with foil, cool in pan.

PINEAPPLE DATE LOAF

1½ cups (240g) chopped pitted dates
125g butter, chopped
450g can crushed pineapple
  in heavy syrup
½ cup (110g) sugar
2 eggs
2 cups (300g) self-raising flour

Grease 15cm x 25cm loaf pan, cover base with baking paper.

Place dates, butter, undrained pineapple and sugar in medium saucepan. Bring to boil, stirring, then simmer, uncovered, 3 minutes; cover, cool.

Stir in eggs and flour. Spoon into prepared pan. Bake in moderately slow oven about 1¼ hours. Stand 10 minutes before turning onto wire rack to cool.

Top cold cake with 1 quantity Cream Cheese Frosting (page 121), if desired.

EASY-MIX BOILED FRUIT CAKE

185g butter, chopped
1kg (5 cups) mixed dried fruit
1 cup (200g) firmly packed
  brown sugar
⅓ cup (80ml) sweet sherry
1 tablespoon coffee and
  chicory essence
½ teaspoon bicarbonate of soda
3 eggs
1½ cups (225g) plain flour
1 tablespoon mixed spice

Line base and side of deep 20cm round cake pan with 3 layers baking paper, bringing paper 5cm above edge of pan.

Place butter, fruit, sugar, sherry and essence in large saucepan. Bring to boil, stirring, then simmer, covered, 5 minutes. Stir in soda; cover, cool.

Stir eggs, flour and spice into mixture, spread into prepared pan. Bake in slow oven about 2½ hours. Cover hot cake tightly with foil, cool in pan.

LAST-MINUTE RICH FRUIT CAKE

250g butter, chopped
1kg (5 cups) mixed dried fruit
1 cup (200g) firmly packed
    brown sugar
½ cup (125ml) brandy
½ cup (125ml) water
½ teaspoon bicarbonate of soda
2 teaspoons grated orange rind
1 teaspoon grated lemon rind
1 tablespoon treacle
5 eggs
1¾ cups (260g) plain flour
⅓ cup (50g) self-raising flour

Grease deep 23cm round cake pan, line base and side with 3 layers of baking paper, bringing paper 5cm above edge of pan.

Place butter, fruit, sugar, brandy and water in large saucepan. Bring to boil, stirring, then simmer, covered, 10 minutes. Stir in soda; cover, cool.

Stir rinds, treacle, eggs and flours into mixture, spread into prepared pan. Decorate with glace cherries and blanched almonds, if desired. Bake in slow oven about 2¾ hours. Cover hot cake tightly with foil, cool in pan.

LEFT: From left: Pineapple Date Loaf, Boiled Pineapple Fruit Cake.
BELOW: From left: Easy-Mix Boiled Fruit Cake, Last-Minute Rich Fruit Cake.

Left: China from Waterford Wedgwood; cake forks from Country Road Homewear; tablecloth from Cottage Manner; tea-towel from Between the Sheets. Below: China from Royal Doulton; tray and serviette from Home & Garden on the Mall; background from Corso de Fiori.

RICH CHOCOLATE HAZELNUT CAKE

125g butter, chopped
125g dark chocolate, chopped
⅔ cup (150g) castor sugar
1 cup (110g) packaged
    ground hazelnuts
1 cup (150g) self-raising flour
4 eggs

Grease deep 20cm round cake pan, cover base with baking paper.

Place butter, chocolate and sugar in medium saucepan, stir over low heat, without boiling, until butter and chocolate are melted; cool 10 minutes. Stir in nuts, flour and eggs. Pour mixture into prepared pan. Bake in moderately slow oven 1 hour. Stand 5 minutes before turning onto wire rack to cool.

Split cold cake in half, fill and decorate with 2 quantities Coffee Liqueur Cream (page 121) and top with chocolate-dipped hazelnuts, if desired.

BELOW: Rich Chocolate Hazelnut Cake.
RIGHT: From left: Spiced Potato Fruit Cake, Raisin and Apple Cake.

Below: Tapestry cushion from Made on Earth.

SPICED POTATO FRUIT CAKE

You will need to cook about 300g potatoes for this cake.

185g butter, chopped
2 tablespoons golden syrup
1 cup (220g) raw sugar
2¾ cups (500g) mixed dried fruit
1 cup cold cooked mashed potato
2 eggs
1 cup (150g) self-raising flour
1 cup (150g) plain flour
1 teaspoon mixed spice
1 teaspoon ground nutmeg

Line base and side of deep 20cm round cake pan with 3 layers of baking paper, bringing paper 5cm above edge of pan.

Place butter, golden syrup, sugar and fruit in medium saucepan. Stir over low heat, without boiling, until butter is melted. Remove from heat, stir in potato and eggs, cover, cool. Stir flours and spices into mixture. Spoon into prepared pan. Bake in moderately slow oven about 2 hours. Cover hot cake tightly with foil, cool in pan.

RAISIN AND APPLE CAKE

2¼ cups (375g) raisins
250g butter, chopped
**1½ cups (300g) firmly packed
    brown sugar**
2 teaspoons ground cinnamon
½ cup (125g) canned pie apples
2 teaspoons instant coffee powder
2 cups (500ml) water
1 egg
3¼ cups (485g) plain flour
2 teaspoons bicarbonate of soda

Grease deep 23cm square cake pan, cover base with baking paper.

Place raisins, butter, sugar, cinnamon, apple, coffee and water in large saucepan. Stir over low heat, without boiling, until butter is melted; cover, cool to room temperature.

Stir egg, flour and soda into raisin mixture. Pour and spread into prepared pan. Bake in moderately slow oven about 1¼ hours. Stand cake 10 minutes before turning onto wire rack to cool.

Top cold cake with 1 quantity Coffee Vienna Cream Frosting (page 121) and sprinkle with chopped walnuts, if desired.

SWEET POTATO AND DATE CAKE

185g butter, chopped
¾ cup (150g) firmly packed
brown sugar
½ cup (80g) chopped pitted dates
1½ cups (200g) grated
uncooked kumara
¼ cup (55g) chopped glace pineapple
2 eggs
1½ cups (225g) self-raising flour
1 teaspoon ground cinnamon

Grease 19cm x 29cm rectangular slice pan, cover base with baking paper.

Combine butter, sugar and dates in medium saucepan, stir over heat, without boiling, until butter is melted; stand 5 minutes. Stir in remaining ingredients. Spread mixture into prepared pan. Bake in moderately slow oven about 45 minutes. Stand 5 minutes before turning onto wire rack to cool.

Top cold cake with 1 quantity Citrus Frosting (page 121), if desired.

TREACLE GINGERBREAD

125g butter, chopped
½ cup (125ml) treacle
⅔ cup (130g) firmly packed
brown sugar
½ cup (125ml) milk
2 eggs
2 cups (300g) self-raising flour
1 tablespoon ground ginger
¼ teaspoon bicarbonate of soda

Grease 23cm square slab cake pan, cover base with baking paper.

Place butter, treacle and sugar in medium saucepan, stir over heat, without boiling, until sugar is dissolved; cool 5 minutes. Stir milk, eggs, flour, ginger and soda into mixture, pour into prepared pan. Bake in moderately slow oven about 45 minutes. Stand 5 minutes before turning onto wire rack to cool.

Top cold cake with 1 quantity Caramel Icing (page 120), and sprinkle with chopped walnuts, if desired.

BOILED GINGER FRUIT CAKE

2 cups (375g) mixed dried fruit
¾ cup (150g) chopped glace ginger
250g butter, chopped
½ cup (100g) firmly packed
    brown sugar
⅓ cup (80ml) golden syrup
½ cup (125ml) sweet sherry
½ teaspoon bicarbonate of soda
2 eggs
1 cup (150g) plain flour
1 cup (150g) self-raising flour
2 teaspoons ground ginger

Line base and sides of deep 19cm square cake pan with 3 layers of baking paper; bringing paper 5cm above edge of pan.

Place fruit, glace ginger, butter, sugar, golden syrup and sherry in large saucepan. Bring to boil, stirring, then simmer, uncovered, 3 minutes. Stir in soda; cover, cool to room temperature.

Stir eggs, flours and ground ginger into mixture, spread into prepared pan. Bake in slow oven about 1¾ hours. Cover hot cake tightly with foil, cool in pan.

LEFT: Sweet Potato and Date Cake.
BELOW: From left: Treacle Gingerbread, Boiled Ginger Fruit Cake.

Left: China from Royal Doulton.
Below: China from Johnson Brothers; tray from House & Garden on the Mall.

95

HONEY AND RAISIN CAKE

125g butter, chopped
½ cup (125ml) honey
¼ cup (55g) raw sugar
2 eggs
½ cup (125ml) milk
1 teaspoon mixed spice
2 cups (300g) self-raising flour
1 cup (170g) raisins

Grease 20cm ring cake pan, cover base with baking paper. Combine butter, honey and sugar in medium saucepan, stir over heat, without boiling, until butter is melted; stand 5 minutes. Stir in remaining ingredients. Pour mixture into prepared pan, bake in moderate oven about 40 minutes. Turn onto wire rack to cool.

Top with 1 quantity Honey Cream Cheese Frosting (page 121), if desired.

ABOVE: From left: Beryl's Boiled Fruit Cake, Honey and Raisin Cake.
RIGHT: Moist Spicy Gingerbread.

Above: China from Johnson Brothers.
Right: China from Lifestyle Imports.

BERYL'S BOILED FRUIT CAKE

2¾ cups (500g) mixed dried fruit
1 cup (220g) sugar
1 cup (250ml) water
185g butter, chopped
1 tablespoon golden syrup
2 teaspoons cocoa
1 teaspoon mixed spice
1 teaspoon instant coffee powder
1 teaspoon bicarbonate of soda
2 eggs
1 cup (150g) self-raising flour
1¼ cups (185g) plain flour

Line base and sides of deep 19cm square cake pan with 3 layers of baking paper, bringing paper 5cm above edge of pan.

Place fruit, sugar, water, butter, golden syrup, cocoa, spice and coffee powder in large saucepan. Bring to boil, stirring, then simmer, uncovered, 10 minutes. Stir in soda; cover, cool to room temperature.

Stir remaining ingredients into mixture, spread into prepared pan. Bake in slow oven about 1½ hours. Cover hot cake tightly with foil, cool in pan.

MOIST SPICY GINGERBREAD

125g butter, chopped
1 cup (250ml) golden syrup
1 cup (220g) castor sugar
2 cups (300g) plain flour
1 teaspoon bicarbonate of soda
2 teaspoons ground ginger
½ teaspoon ground cinnamon
½ teaspoon mixed spice
¼ teaspoon ground cloves
2 eggs
¾ cup (180ml) milk

Grease 23cm square slab cake pan, line base and sides with baking paper.

Place butter and golden syrup in medium saucepan, stir over heat until butter is melted. Stir in sugar, flour, soda, spices, eggs and milk. Pour into prepared pan. Bake in moderately slow oven about 1 hour. Stand 5 minutes before turning onto wire rack to cool.

Top cold cake with 1 quantity Lemon Vienna Cream Frosting (page 121), if desired.

Spoon Method

All you need is a bowl and a wooden spoon to create a stirring success with any of these popular fruit cakes, carrot cakes, chocolate cakes, and more; they're great for all kinds of occasions.

OUR TIPS FOR SUCCESS

- Using a wooden spoon, simply stir all ingredients together in a bowl.

- With the wooden spoon, beat the mixtures quite vigorously, except for the richer, heavier fruit cakes, until all the ingredients are combined.

- The rich fruit cakes are too dense to beat, but stir them well to be sure the ingredients are thoroughly combined.

WHOLEMEAL HONEY DATE CAKE

125g butter, melted
2 tablespoons honey
½ cup (110g) raw sugar
1 egg
1½ cups (240g) chopped pitted dates
⅔ cup (160ml) milk
½ cup (80g) wholemeal
    self-raising flour
1 cup (150g) white self-raising flour

Grease 15cm x 25cm loaf pan, cover base with baking paper.

Combine all ingredients in medium bowl, stir until combined. Spread mixture into prepared pan. Bake in moderate oven about 50 minutes. Stand 10 minutes before turning onto wire rack to cool.

ORANGE COCONUT CAKE

125g butter, melted
1 tablespoon grated orange rind
1 cup (220g) castor sugar
½ cup (45g) coconut
2 eggs
1 cup (250ml) milk
1½ cups (225g) self-raising flour

Grease 14cm x 21cm loaf pan, line base and sides with baking paper.

Combine all ingredients in medium bowl, stir until well combined. Pour mixture into prepared pan. Bake in moderate oven about 1¼ hours. Turn onto wire rack to cool.

Top cold cake with 1 quantity Vienna Cream Frosting (page 121) and sprinkle with toasted shredded coconut (page 122), if desired.

RIGHT: From left: Orange Coconut Cake, Wholemeal Honey Date Cake.

Basket from Made on Earth; plate and jug from On Broadway Antique Market.

CARROT COCONUT CAKE

You will need about 300g carrots.

1½ cups finely grated carrot, firmly packed
3 eggs
1 cup (250ml) vegetable oil
1 cup (200g) firmly packed brown sugar
½ cup (45g) coconut
½ cup (80g) sultanas
2 cups (300g) self-raising flour
1 teaspoon mixed spice

Grease 23cm square slab cake pan, cover base with baking paper.

Combine all ingredients in medium bowl, stir until combined. Spread mixture into prepared pan. Bake in moderately slow oven about 50 minutes. Stand cake 10 minutes before turning onto wire rack to cool.

Top cold cake with 1 quantity Caramel Icing (page 120), and sprinkle with toasted shredded coconut (page 122), if desired.

SOUR CREAM CARROT CAKE

You will need about 300g carrots.

1½ cups finely grated carrot, firmly packed
1 cup (150g) white plain flour
1 cup (160g) wholemeal self-raising flour
1 teaspoon bicarbonate of soda
2 teaspoons ground cinnamon
2 teaspoons ground nutmeg
1 cup (200g) firmly packed brown sugar
4 eggs
½ cup (125ml) sour cream
1 cup (250ml) vegetable oil

Grease deep 23cm round cake pan, cover base with baking paper.

Combine all ingredients in large bowl, stir until mixture is well combined. Pour mixture into prepared pan. Bake in moderately slow oven about 1 hour. Stand 10 minutes before turning onto wire rack to cool.

BELOW: From left: Sour Cream Carrot Cake, Carrot Coconut Cake.
RIGHT: From left: Pecan Candy Cake, Rich Honeyed Fruit Cake.

Below: China from Waterford Wedgwood; basket from Morris Home & Garden Wares; tapestry in background from Parker's of Turramurra.
Right: Cherub from Made on Earth.

PECAN CANDY CAKE

½ cup (125g) halved glace cherries
½ cup (115g) chopped glace
  pineapple
¾ cup (120g) chopped pitted dates
1¾ cups (175g) pecans
¾ cup (50g) shredded coconut
1 tablespoon self-raising flour
⅔ cup (160ml) sweetened
  condensed milk

Grease 8cm x 26cm bar cake pan, line base and sides with baking paper.

Combine all ingredients in medium bowl, stir until well combined. Spoon mixture into prepared pan, press down firmly. Bake in slow oven about 1 hour. Cover hot cake tightly with foil, cool in pan. Serve thinly sliced.

RICH HONEYED FRUIT CAKE

1kg (5 cups) mixed dried fruit
3 eggs
⅓ cup (80ml) honey
1¼ cups (185g) plain flour

Grease deep 23cm round cake pan, line base and side with baking paper.

Combine all ingredients in large bowl, stir until well combined. Spread mixture into prepared pan. Bake in slow oven about 1¼ hours. Cover hot cake tightly with foil, cool in pan.

When cake is cold, drizzle with melted chocolate, if desired. Serve thinly sliced.

FRUITY TEA LOAF

1 cup (150g) currants
1 cup (160g) sultanas
1 cup (170g) chopped raisins
¼ cup (40g) mixed peel
1 cup (200g) firmly packed
    brown sugar
1 cup (250ml) strong cold
    strained tea
1 tablespoon sherry
1 egg
1 cup (150g) plain flour
1 cup (150g) self-raising flour

Grease 15cm x 25cm loaf pan, cover base with baking paper.

Combine all ingredients in medium bowl, stir until well combined. Pour into prepared pan. Bake in moderately slow oven about 1½ hours. Cover hot cake tightly with foil, cool in pan.

EASY-MIX FRUIT CAKE

250g butter, melted
2 teaspoons grated lemon rind
1¼ cups (250g) firmly packed
    brown sugar
2¾ cups (500g) mixed dried fruit
⅓ cup (80ml) brandy
¼ cup (60ml) lemon juice
4 eggs
1 cup (150g) self-raising flour
1 cup (150g) plain flour
1 teaspoon mixed spice

Line base and side of deep 20cm round cake pan with 3 layers of baking paper, bringing paper 5cm above edge of pan.

Combine all ingredients in large bowl, stir until well combined. Pour mixture into prepared pan. Bake in slow oven about 2 hours. Cover hot cake tightly with foil, cool in pan.

ABOVE: From left: Fruity Tea Loaf, Easy-Mix Fruit Cake.

Tray and wreath from Made on Earth.

SOUR CREAM CHOC-ORANGE CAKE

100g dark chocolate, melted
125g butter, melted
1 tablespoon grated orange rind
1 cup (200g) firmly packed
   brown sugar
2 eggs
¾ cup (180ml) sour cream
½ cup (125ml) marmalade
1 cup (150g) plain flour
1 cup (150g) self-raising flour
½ teaspoon bicarbonate of soda
2 tablespoons cocoa

Grease 23cm square slab cake pan, cover base and sides with baking paper.

Combine all ingredients in medium bowl, stir until well combined. Spoon mixture into prepared pan. Bake in moderate oven about 45 minutes. Turn onto wire rack to cool.

Top cold cake with 1 quantity Orange Vienna Cream Frosting (page 121), if desired.

DOUBLE CHOCOLATE CAKE

60g dark chocolate, melted
125g butter, melted
1¼ cups (185g) self-raising flour
¾ cup (110g) plain flour
1 cup (220g) castor sugar
⅓ cup (65g) firmly packed
   brown sugar
2 tablespoons cocoa
½ teaspoon bicarbonate of soda
2 eggs
¾ cup (180ml) milk

Grease deep 23cm round cake pan, cover base with paper.

Combine all ingredients in medium bowl, stir until well combined. Spoon mixture into prepared pan. Bake in moderate oven about 45 minutes. Turn onto wire rack to cool.

Top cold cake with 1 quantity Caramel Icing (page 120) sprinkled with chopped hazelnuts, if desired.

BELOW: From back: Double Chocolate Cake, Sour Cream Choc-Orange Cake.

China from Waterford Wedgwood.

"Rub In" Method

All you do is rub the butter into the flour until the mixture looks like coarse breadcrumbs, then add other ingredients as specified. The result is cakes with firm, moist textures and good flavour; some are served with butter.

OUR TIPS FOR SUCCESS

- Butter should be firm from the refrigerator, and chopped for easy handling.
- Use your fingertips to rub the butter into the flour, etc.
- Pick up a few small pieces of butter and plenty of flour between fingertips and thumbs. Gently but quickly rub the butter into the flour, squashing the pieces of butter lightly as you do so. Shake the bowl so the unrubbed pieces of butter come to the surface. When the mixture looks like coarse breadcrumbs, stop; don't over-handle the crumbs.
- After adding the remaining ingredients, stir together only until combined; mixtures should look coarse and lumpy and are mostly fairly moist.

MOIST APPLE SULTANA CAKE

Cake is best made on day of serving.

¾ cup (110g) self-raising flour
¾ cup (110g) plain flour
125g butter, chopped
**1½ cups (300g) firmly packed
   brown sugar**
¾ cup (180g) canned pie apples
1 cup (160g) sultanas
½ teaspoon bicarbonate of soda
1 teaspoon mixed spice
1 egg
¾ cup (180ml) milk

Grease 19cm x 29cm rectangular slab cake pan, line base and sides with baking paper.

Place flours into large bowl, rub in butter with fingertips, stir in sugar. Press half the mixture over base of prepared pan, carefully spread with apple, sprinkle with sultanas. Add soda, spice, egg and milk to remaining mixture in bowl, stir to combine, pour into pan. Bake in moderate oven about 55 minutes. Stand few minutes before turning onto wire rack to cool upside down.

Dust cold cake with sifted icing sugar, if desired.

RIGHT: Moist Apple Sultana Cake.

Apple stand from Accoutrement.

BRANDIED LIGHT FRUIT CAKE

1¼ cups (185g) plain flour
1¼ cups (185g) self-raising flour
185g butter, chopped
4 cups (750g) mixed dried fruit
¾ cup (165g) raw sugar
¾ cup (180ml) hot milk
2 tablespoons brandy
2 eggs

Line base and side of deep 20cm round cake pan with 3 layers of baking paper, bringing paper 5cm above edge of pan.

Combine flours in large bowl, rub in butter with fingertips. Stir in remaining ingredients. Spread mixture into prepared pan. Bake in slow oven about 2½ hours. Cover hot cake tightly with foil, cool in pan.

ONE-EGG SULTANA CHERRY CAKE

2½ cups (375g) plain flour
½ cup (75g) self-raising flour
1 teaspoon bicarbonate of soda
250g butter, chopped
1 cup (200g) firmly packed
    brown sugar
1½ cups (240g) sultanas
⅔ cup (140g) glace cherries, halved
1 egg
¾ cup (180ml) milk
¼ cup (60ml) white vinegar

Line base and sides of deep 19cm square cake pan with 3 layers of baking paper, bringing paper 5cm above edge of pan.

Combine flours and soda in large bowl,

rub in butter with fingertips. Stir in sugar, sultanas and cherries, then egg, milk and vinegar. Spread mixture into prepared pan. Bake in slow oven about 2 hours. Cover hot cake tightly with foil, cool in pan.

ABOVE: From left: Brandied Light Fruit Cake, One-Egg Sultana Cherry Cake.

China from Royal Copenhagen; box from Sandy de Beyer.

106

OVERNIGHT DATE CAKE

1¾ cups (260g) self-raising flour
1 teaspoon bicarbonate of soda
60g butter, chopped
½ cup (110g) castor sugar
2 cups (320g) chopped pitted dates
1 cup (250ml) milk

Grease 14cm x 21cm loaf pan, cover base with baking paper.

Place flour and soda in large bowl, rub in butter with fingertips. Stir in sugar, dates and milk. Cover bowl, stand overnight.

Spread mixture into prepared pan. Bake in moderately slow oven about 1¼ hours. Stand 10 minutes before turning onto wire rack to cool.

BELOW: Overnight Date Cake.

China from Waterford Wedgwood; butter box from Cottage Manner.

SPICY FRUIT LOAF

2 cups (300g) plain flour
1 teaspoon bicarbonate of soda
¼ teaspoon ground nutmeg
¼ teaspoon ground ginger
½ teaspoon mixed spice
125g butter, chopped
1 cup (200g) firmly packed
   brown sugar
2¾ cups (500g) mixed dried fruit
1 egg
1 cup (250ml) milk

Grease 15cm x 25cm loaf pan, cover base with baking paper.

Place flour, soda and spices into large bowl, rub in butter with fingertips. Stir in sugar and fruit, then egg and milk; mixture should look lumpy. Spread mixture into prepared pan. Bake in moderate oven about 1¼ hours. Stand 10 minutes before turning onto wire rack to cool.

FRUITY GINGERBREAD

1¾ cups (260g) plain flour
1 teaspoon bicarbonate of soda
1 tablespoon ground ginger
125g butter, chopped
¾ cup (150g) firmly packed
   brown sugar
½ cup (95g) mixed dried fruit
2 teaspoons grated orange rind
2 tablespoons mixed peel
1 egg
⅓ cup (80ml) golden syrup
¾ cup (180ml) milk

Grease 19cm x 29cm rectangular slab cake pan, cover base with baking paper.

Place flour, soda and ginger into large bowl, rub in butter with fingertips. Stir in sugar, fruit, rind and peel, egg, golden syrup and milk; mixture should look lumpy. Spread into prepared pan. Bake in moderate oven about 45 minutes. Stand 5 minutes before turning onto wire rack to cool.

Dust cold cake with sifted icing sugar, if desired.

GOLDEN PUMPKIN LOAF

You will need to cook about 200g peeled, seeded pumpkin for this loaf.

2 cups (300g) self-raising flour
½ teaspoon ground cinnamon
¼ teaspoon ground nutmeg
¼ teaspoon ground ginger
125g butter, chopped
½ cup (110g) castor sugar
½ cup (85g) raisins, chopped
2 eggs
¼ cup (60ml) milk
1 tablespoon vegetable oil
½ cup cold cooked mashed pumpkin

Grease 15cm x 25cm loaf pan, cover base with baking paper.

Place flour and spices into large bowl, rub in butter with fingertips. Stir in sugar and raisins, then eggs, milk, oil and pumpkin; mixture should look lumpy. Spread mixture into prepared pan. Bake in moderate oven about 50 minutes. Turn onto wire rack to cool.

Top cold cake with 1 quantity Orange Vienna Cream Frosting (page 121), and decorate with orange shreds (page 123), if desired.

LEFT: From left: Spicy Fruit Loaf, Fruity Gingerbread.

ABOVE: Golden Pumpkin Loaf.

Above: All-white china from Waterford Wedgwood; duck scoop from Cottage Manner.

Blender or Processor

It's very convenient to mix these cakes in a large blender, a food processor or a jug using a hand-held food processor. However, appliances vary in what they can do, so always check the manufacturer's instructions before you start.

OUR TIPS FOR SUCCESS

- **If using a blender:** To be sure all the ingredients are combined, it is necessary to stop and start the machine often, about every 5 or 10 seconds, and scrape the mixture down from the side of the container so it comes in contact with the blades. Once all the ingredients have been combined, a few short bursts of power will be enough to mix the ingredients thoroughly.

- Do not operate a blender for long periods of time as some of the smaller types can over-heat. As a guide, operate continuously for up to 30 seconds only.

- **If using a food processor:** It is necessary to process the ingredients until they are combined. Do this either by using the pulse action, or by turning the machine off and on in short bursts. It will be necessary to scrape the mixture from the side of the bowl during this process. After the ingredients are combined, process the mixture until it is thoroughly mixed; this will take about 30 seconds to 1 minute.

- **If using a hand-held food processor:** It is important to place ingredients in a fairly tall and narrow receptacle; a large, straight-sided jug is ideal. Mix the ingredients together using the processor in an up-and-down action. Mix until all ingredients are well combined.

- Ingredients should be at room temperature, particularly butter.

CHOCOLATE APPLE CAKE

185g butter, chopped
1¼ cups (275g) castor sugar
3 eggs
2 cups (300g) self-raising flour
⅓ cup (35g) cocoa
¼ teaspoon bicarbonate of soda
⅓ cup (80ml) water
2 medium (about 300g) apples,
    peeled, cored, chopped

Grease deep 20cm round cake pan, line base and side with baking paper.

Combine all ingredients in large jug or bowl of processor or blender. Mix until ingredients are well combined, scraping side of container occasionally. Spread mixture into prepared pan. Bake in moderate oven about 1¼ hours. Stand few minutes before turning onto wire rack to cool.

Top cold cake with 1 quantity Rich Chocolate Glace Icing (page 120), and chocolate curls (page 122), if desired.

Alternative Method: Chocolate Apple Cake can also be made by the One Bowl Method (see page 2).

Combine all ingredients, except apples, in medium bowl, beat with electric mixer until smooth and changed in colour. Stir in apples. Then proceed as directed in recipe.

RIGHT: Chocolate Apple Cake.

Apple stand from Made on Earth.

CHOCOLATE CAKE

125g butter, chopped
¾ cup (165g) castor sugar
2 eggs
1¼ cups (185g) self-raising flour
¼ cup (25g) cocoa
¾ cup (180ml) milk

Grease 20cm ring cake pan, cover base with baking paper.

Combine all ingredients in large jug or bowl of processor or blender. Mix until ingredients are well combined, scraping side of container occasionally. Pour mixture into prepared pan. Bake in moderate oven about 40 minutes. Turn onto wire rack to cool.

Top cold cake with 1 quantity Milk Chocolate Icing (page 120), if desired.

Alternative Method: Chocolate Cake can also be made by the One Bowl Method (see page 2).

Combine all ingredients in medium bowl, beat with electric mixer until smooth and changed in colour. Then proceed as directed in recipe.

ABOVE: Orange Cake.
RIGHT: Chocolate Cake.
FAR RIGHT: Carrot Pineapple Cake.

Above and right: China from Villeroy & Boch.
Far right: Board and egg basket from
On Broadway Antique Market.

ORANGE CAKE

60g butter, chopped
3 teaspoons grated orange rind
1 cup (220g) castor sugar
2 eggs
1 cup (150g) self-raising flour
2 tablespoons plain flour
⅓ cup (80ml) milk

Grease 14cm x 21cm loaf pan, line base and sides with baking paper.

Combine all ingredients in large jug or bowl of processor or blender. Mix until ingredients are well combined, scraping side of container occasionally. Pour mixture into prepared pan. Bake in moderate oven about 40 minutes. Turn onto wire rack to cool.

Top cold cake with 1 quantity Passionfruit Cream Cheese Frosting (page 121), if desired.

Alternative Method: Orange Cake can also be made by the One Bowl Method (see page 2).

Combine all ingredients in small bowl, beat with electric mixer until mixture is smooth and changed in colour. Then proceed as directed in recipe.

CARROT PINEAPPLE CAKE

You need about 250g carrots for this cake. A large blender is required to hold the mixture.

3 eggs
½ cup (125ml) vegetable oil
¾ cup (180ml) plain yogurt
1¾ cups (260g) self-raising flour
¾ cup (165g) castor sugar
1 teaspoon bicarbonate of soda
1½ cups coarsely grated carrot
½ cup (60g) packaged
**   ground almonds**
⅔ cup (60g) coconut
½ cup well-drained canned
**   crushed pineapple in syrup**

Grease 23cm square slab cake pan, cover base with baking paper.

Combine all ingredients in large jug or bowl of processor or large blender. Mix until ingredients are well combined, scraping side of container occasionally. Pour mixture into prepared pan. Bake in moderate oven about 50 minutes. Turn onto wire rack to cool.

Top cold cake with 1 quantity Honey Cream Cheese Frosting (page 121), if desired.

Alternative Method: Carrot Pineapple Cake can also be made by the Spoon Method (see page 98).

Combine all ingredients in large bowl, stir with wooden spoon until combined. Then proceed as directed in recipe.

Muffins

Any time is muffin time! They're popular for breakfast, brunch and snacks, or simply with tea or coffee. Eat muffins hot, warm or cold, with or without butter; they are best made on the day of serving. Each recipe makes 12.

OUR TIPS FOR SUCCESS

■ We used a medium-sized muffin pan (1/3 cup/80ml capacity). Larger and smaller pans are available, but you will need to adjust baking times if you use these pans. Pans should be slightly more than half-filled with mixture, whatever size muffin pans are used.

■ Pans should be greased evenly or coated with a non-stick spray.

■ Butter should be firm from the refrigerator when it is to be chopped.

■ Mixtures require minimum mixing and should look coarse and lumpy. We found a large metal spoon or fork the best implement to use.

■ To test if muffins are cooked, they should be browned, risen, firm to touch and beginning to shrink from sides of pan. Turn muffins from the pan onto a wire rack as soon as they are cooked to prevent them becoming steamy.

■ Cold muffins freeze well. For easy thawing, wrap individually in foil.

■ To thaw in a conventional oven, place foil-wrapped muffins in a single layer on an oven tray in a moderate oven for about 20 minutes or until they reach the right eating temperature for you.

■ To thaw in a microwave oven, remove foil, place muffins in a single layer in the oven, microwave on full power for about 40 seconds per muffin or until heated.

APPLE AND CUSTARD MUFFINS

90g butter, melted
2 cups (300g) self-raising flour
1 cup (150g) plain flour
1/2 teaspoon ground cinnamon
3/4 cup (165g) castor sugar
1 egg
1 cup (250ml) milk
1/4 cup (60ml) thick packaged custard
1/2 cup (125g) canned pie apples
2 tablespoons brown sugar
1/2 teaspoon ground cinnamon, extra

Grease 12 hole muffin pan (1/3 cup/80ml capacity). Combine butter, flours, cinnamon, castor sugar, egg and milk in large bowl, stir with large metal spoon until just combined. Divide half the mixture into prepared pan, make a well in centre of each muffin, drop 1 level teaspoon custard and 2 level teaspoons apple into each well. Top with remaining mixture, sprinkle with combined brown sugar and extra cinnamon. Bake in moderately hot oven about 25 minutes. Turn onto wire rack.

FRESH BLUEBERRY MUFFINS

200g fresh blueberries
2 cups (300g) self-raising flour
1 cup (150g) plain flour
1 1/2 teaspoons mixed spice
1/2 teaspoon bicarbonate of soda
1 cup (200g) firmly packed
   brown sugar
1 egg
1 1/3 cups (330ml) milk
1/3 cup (80ml) vegetable oil

Grease 12 hole muffin pan (1/3 cup/80ml capacity). Reserve 1/4 cup blueberries. Combine remaining blueberries with remaining ingredients in large bowl, stir with large metal spoon until just combined. Spoon mixture into prepared pan, press reserved blueberries on top. Bake in moderately hot oven about 20 minutes. Turn onto wire rack.

RIGHT: In basket, from left: Apple and Custard Muffins, Fresh Blueberry Muffins.

CHEESE AND CHIVE MUFFINS

2¼ cups (335g) self-raising flour
1½ tablespoons castor sugar
50g butter, chopped
¾ cup (60g) coarsely grated
    parmesan cheese
3 teaspoons dry mustard
¼ cup chopped fresh chives
1 egg
1 cup (250ml) milk
½ cup (40g) coarsely grated
    parmesan cheese, extra

Grease 12 hole muffin pan (⅓ cup/80ml capacity). Combine flour and sugar in large bowl, rub in butter. Add cheese, mustard, chives, egg and milk, stir with large metal spoon until just combined. Spoon mixture into prepared pan, sprinkle with extra cheese. Bake in moderately hot oven about 20 minutes. Turn onto wire rack.

CURRIED PUMPKIN MUFFINS

You will need to cook 400g peeled, seeded pumpkin for these muffins.

2 cups (300g) self-raising flour
1 cup (150g) plain flour
1 teaspoon bicarbonate of soda
2 teaspoons castor sugar
2 teaspoons ground cumin
2 teaspoons ground coriander
½ teaspoon salt
½ cup (60g) bacon-flavoured chips
1 cup cold cooked
    mashed pumpkin
2 tablespoons hot vindaloo
    curry paste
1 egg
¼ cup (60ml) vegetable oil
1 cup (250ml) milk

Grease 12 hole muffin pan (⅓ cup/80ml capacity). Combine all ingredients in large bowl, stir with large metal spoon until just combined. Spoon mixture into prepared pan. Bake in moderately hot oven about 25 minutes. Turn onto wire rack.

ABOVE: From left: Cheese and Chive Muffins, Curried Pumpkin Muffins.

China from Waterford Wedgwood.

APRICOT COCONUT MUFFINS

2 cups (300g) self-raising flour
125g butter, chopped
¾ cup (165g) castor sugar
1 cup (150g) chopped dried apricots
1 cup (90g) coconut
¾ cup (180ml) milk
2 eggs

Grease 12 hole muffin pan (⅓ cup/80ml capacity). Place flour in large bowl, rub in butter. Add remaining ingredients, stir with large metal spoon until just combined. Spoon mixture into prepared pan. Bake in moderately hot oven about 20 minutes. Turn onto wire rack.

HAZELNUT PLUM MUFFINS

90g butter, melted
2½ cups (375g) self-raising flour
½ cup (55g) ground hazelnuts
⅔ cup (150g) castor sugar
1 egg
1 cup (250ml) milk
½ cup (125ml) plum jam

Grease 12 hole muffin pan (⅓ cup/80ml capacity). Combine butter, flour, nuts, sugar, egg and milk in large bowl, stir with large metal spoon until just combined. Half-fill prepared pan with mixture, make small well in centre of each muffin, spoon 2 teaspoons jam into each well, top with remaining muffin mixture. Bake in moderately hot oven about 25 minutes. Turn onto wire rack carefully, as jam is hot.

BELOW: From left: Hazelnut Plum Muffins, Apricot Coconut Muffins.

FRUIT 'N' SPICE MUFFINS

3 cups (450g) self-raising flour
2 teaspoons mixed spice
½ cup (110g) castor sugar
125g butter, chopped
¾ cup (180ml) milk
2 eggs
1 cup (190g) mixed dried fruit

Grease 12 hole muffin pan (⅓ cup/80ml capacity). Combine flour, spice and sugar in large bowl, rub in butter. Add milk, eggs and fruit, stir with large metal spoon until just combined. Spoon mixture into prepared pan. Bake in moderately hot oven about 25 minutes. Turn onto wire rack.

OVERNIGHT DATE AND MUESLI MUFFINS

Muffins are better if mixture is allowed to stand overnight.

1¼ cups (185g) plain flour
1¼ cups (160g) toasted muesli
1 teaspoon ground cinnamon
1 teaspoon bicarbonate of soda
½ cup (100g) firmly packed
**   brown sugar**
½ cup (40g) unprocessed bran
¾ cup (120g) chopped pitted dates
1½ cups (375ml) buttermilk
½ cup (125ml) vegetable oil
1 egg

Grease 12 hole muffin pan (⅓ cup/80ml capacity). Combine all ingredients in large bowl, stir with large metal spoon until just combined. Cover, refrigerate overnight. Spoon mixture into prepared pan. Bake in moderately hot oven about 25 minutes. Turn onto wire rack.

WHOLEMEAL DATE AND BANANA MUFFINS

You will need about 3 over-ripe medium bananas for these muffins.

1½ cups (240g) wholemeal
**   self-raising flour**
60g butter, chopped
1 tablespoon raw sugar
1 cup (160g) finely chopped
**   pitted dates**
1 cup mashed banana
2 eggs
2 tablespoons milk

Grease 12 hole muffin pan (⅓ cup/80ml capacity). Place flour in large bowl, rub in butter. Add remaining ingredients, stir with large metal spoon until just combined. Spoon mixture into prepared pan. Bake in moderately hot oven about 25 minutes. Turn onto wire rack.

ABOVE LEFT: Triple Treat Chocolate Muffins.

RIGHT: Clockwise from top: Wholemeal Date and Banana Muffins, Fruit 'n' Spice Muffins, Overnight Date and Muesli Muffins.

Above left: Sugar bowl and serviette rings from Home & Garden on the Mall.

TRIPLE TREAT CHOCOLATE MUFFINS

90g butter, melted
2½ cups (375g) self-raising flour
½ cup (50g) cocoa
¾ cup (165g) castor sugar
1 egg
1⅓ cups (330ml) milk
¾ cup (130g) chopped
**   white chocolate**
½ cup (90g) chopped milk chocolate

Grease 12 hole muffin pan (⅓ cup/80ml capacity). Combine all ingredients in large bowl, stir with large metal spoon until just combined. Spoon mixture into prepared pan. Bake in moderately hot oven about 25 minutes. Turn onto wire rack.

Icings, Frostings and Fillings

On these pages are all the icings, frostings and fillings we used in this book; they are simple to make.

OUR TIPS FOR SUCCESS

- Ice, frost or fill cakes which have been cooled to room temperature for best results.
- Where we say "stir over hot water", we mean you to place the heatproof bowl over a saucepan of hot water or in a sink of hot water.
- Stir mixtures with a wooden spoon.
- Butter and cream cheese should be soft (not melted) in these recipes.
- Cream for whipping should be very cold, straight from the refrigerator.
- You can tint icings and frostings with food colourings, if desired.
- Use a palette knife or spatula to spread icings, fillings and frostings.
- You will find more helpful tips and techniques on the next pages.

GLACE ICING

1½ cups (240g) icing sugar mixture
1 teaspoon soft butter
2 tablespoons milk, approximately

Sift icing sugar into small heatproof bowl, stir in butter and enough milk to give a firm paste. Stir over hot water until icing is spreadable; do not over-heat. Spread icing over cold cake immediately.

VARIATIONS

Chocolate: Add 2 or 3 tablespoons cocoa to icing sugar when sifting.
Coffee: Add 3 teaspoons instant coffee powder to icing sugar when sifting.
Lemon: Substitute lemon juice for milk; 1 teaspoon grated rind can be added, if desired.
Maple Syrup: Substitute maple syrup for milk.
Orange: Substitute orange juice for milk; 1 teaspoon grated rind can be added, if desired.
Passionfruit: Add the pulp of 1 passionfruit and enough milk to give a spreadable consistency.

CARAMEL ICING

60g butter
½ cup (100g) firmly packed brown sugar
2 tablespoons milk
¾ cup (120g) icing sugar mixture, approximately

Melt butter in small saucepan, add brown sugar and milk, bring to boil, then simmer, stirring, 2 minutes; cool. Stir in enough sifted icing sugar to give a spreadable consistency.

RICH CHOCOLATE GLACE ICING

90g dark chocolate, chopped
1 teaspoon vegetable oil
¼ cup (60ml) water
2 cups (320g) icing sugar mixture, approximately

Combine chocolate, oil and water in medium saucepan, stir over low heat until chocolate is melted. Gradually beat in enough sifted icing sugar to give a smooth, spreading consistency.

MILK CHOCOLATE ICING

125g dark chocolate, chopped
60g butter
2 tablespoons sweetened condensed milk

Combine chocolate, butter and milk in small heatproof bowl, stir over hot water until smooth; cool. Beat icing with electric mixer until mixture thickens and changes slightly in colour.

CHOCOLATE BUTTER CREAM

125g unsalted butter, chopped
125g dark chocolate, chopped

Melt butter and chocolate in small heatproof bowl over hot water, cool to room temperature. Beat with wooden spoon until thick and spreadable.

CHOCOLATE GLAZE

150g dark chocolate, chopped
30g butter
2 teaspoons vegetable oil

Combine all ingredients in small heatproof bowl, stir over hot water until smooth; use while warm.

CHOCOLATE CREAM TOPPING

½ cup (125ml) thickened cream
125g dark chocolate, chopped

Heat cream in small saucepan until boiling, remove from heat; add chocolate, stir until smooth. Cool until thick and pourable.

SOUR CREAM CHOCOLATE GLAZE

100g dark chocolate, chopped
60g unsalted butter
½ cup (80g) icing sugar mixture
¼ cup (60ml) sour cream

Combine all ingredients in small saucepan, stir over low heat until smooth. Bring to boil, simmer, uncovered, 2 minutes; cool 5 minutes before using.

VIENNA CREAM FROSTING

125g butter, chopped
1½ cups (240g) icing sugar mixture
2 tablespoons milk

Beat butter in small bowl with electric mixer until as white as possible. Gradually beat in half the sifted icing sugar, all the milk, then remaining icing sugar.

VARIATIONS

Chocolate: Sift 2 or 3 tablespoons cocoa with the icing sugar; add a little more milk, if necessary.
Cinnamon: Sift 2 teaspoons ground cinnamon with the icing sugar.
Coffee: Dissolve 3 teaspoons instant coffee powder in 2 tablespoons hot water; cool. Substitute for milk.
Lemon: Substitute lemon juice for milk; 1 teaspoon grated rind can be added.
Orange: Substitute orange juice for milk; 1 teaspoon grated rind can be added.

CREAM CHEESE FROSTING

90g packaged cream
cheese, chopped
90g butter, chopped
1 cup (160g) icing sugar mixture

Beat cheese and butter in small bowl with electric mixer until as white as possible. Gradually beat in sifted icing sugar.

VARIATIONS

Choc-Hazelnut: Reduce cream cheese and butter to 60g each, and beat in 2 tablespoons hazelnut spread with cheese and butter.
Golden: Beat in 2 tablespoons golden syrup with cheese and butter.
Honey: Beat in 1 tablespoon honey with cheese and butter.
Passionfruit: Reduce cream cheese and butter to 60g each, and stir in the pulp of 1 passionfruit after beating in icing sugar.
Treacle: Beat in 1 tablespoon treacle with cheese and butter.

CITRUS FROSTING

1½ cups (240g) icing sugar mixture
1 teaspoon grated orange
or lemon rind
30g soft butter
1½ tablespoons orange
or lemon juice, approximately

Combine sifted icing sugar, rind and butter in small bowl, stir in enough juice to give a spreadable consistency.

CHOCOLATE FUDGE FROSTING

45g unsalted butter
2 tablespoons water
¼ cup (55g) castor sugar
¾ cup (120g) icing sugar mixture
2 tablespoons cocoa

Combine butter, water and castor sugar in small saucepan, stir over heat, without boiling, until sugar is dissolved. Sift icing sugar and cocoa into small heatproof bowl, gradually stir in hot butter mixture; cover, refrigerate until thick. Beat with wooden spoon until mixture is smooth and spreadable.

CHANTILLY CREAM

300ml thickened cream
1 tablespoon castor sugar
½ teaspoon vanilla essence

Combine all ingredients in small bowl, beat with rotary beater or electric mixer until soft peaks form.

PASSIONFRUIT CREAM

300ml thickened cream
1 tablespoon castor sugar
2 passionfruit

Beat cream and sugar in small bowl with rotary beater or electric mixer until soft peaks form, fold in passionfruit pulp.

LIQUEUR CREAM

Any favourite liqueur can be used in this cream.

300ml thickened cream
1 tablespoon liqueur
1 tablespoon icing sugar mixture

Beat cream, liqueur and sugar in small bowl with rotary beater or electric mixer until soft peaks form.

VARIATIONS

Coffee: Use 1 tablespoon Kahlua and 2 teaspoons instant coffee powder dissolved in 1 teaspoon water.
Chocolate: Use 1 tablespoon Creme de Cacao and 2 teaspoons cocoa dissolved in 1 teaspoon water.

Throughout this book, we have used Namco aluminium cake pans.

TO GREASE AND LINE PANS

We use melted butter and a pastry brush or non-stick sprays to grease cake pans and muffin pans evenly. For richer cakes, we lined the side/s and base with 3 layers of baking paper (page 123); greaseproof or brown paper can also be used.

OVENS AND COOKING TIMES

Be guided by the oven manufacturer's instructions. It is best to "get to know your oven" and adjust shelves and temperatures accordingly. Many domestic ovens brown unevenly. If necessary, turn the cake during cooking time; if this is done quickly, it will not hurt the cake. If a cake is browning too quickly on top, cover with brown paper or foil.

For a fan-forced or convection oven, follow the manufacturer's instructions. None of these cakes was created for a microwave oven, nor tested in one.

TO TEST IF CAKES ARE COOKED

After the suggested cooking time, the cake should be browned and starting to shrink from the sides of the pan. Feel the top with your fingertips; it should feel firm. Then, insert a thin skewer into the thickest part of the cake, to the base of the pan. The skewer should be free from mixture. Do not confuse with stickiness from fruit.

COOLING CAKES

We have suggested standing cakes for times of up to 10 minutes before turning onto wire racks to cool. The best way to handle a hot cake is to allow it to stand, as directed, then hold the pan firmly and shake gently to free the cake from the pan.

Turn the cake onto a wire rack, then turn the cake right way up using another wire rack, unless directed otherwise. We have indicated when it is best to cool cakes in pans; these are always covered with foil before cooling, and are mostly fruit cakes.

KEEPING TIMES

Most cakes will keep in an airtight container at room temperature for a few days, or up to a week in the refrigerator. Rich fruit cakes will keep for a month. Cakes must be well wrapped to exclude air and light. We use plastic wrap, then foil.

All cakes freeze well; they are best frozen uniced and unfilled. They must always be well wrapped.

All the Trimmings

You can quickly decorate your cakes with these easy ideas using chocolate, nuts, coconut, citrus peel and feather and fan design. We also tell you how to line cake pans and make a paper piping bag for adding special finishing touches.

HOW TO MELT CHOCOLATE

Chocolate should never be melted by itself over direct heat. Instead, use a double saucepan or a heatproof bowl over a saucepan of water. Place roughly chopped chocolate in the top half of the saucepan or the bowl.

Add water to the bottom half of the saucepan, but not enough to touch the base of the top saucepan or bowl. Bring water to the boil, remove from heat, then immediately place the chocolate in its saucepan or bowl over the hot water. Stand, stirring occasionally, until the chocolate is smooth.

Do not cover the bowl containing the chocolate or condensation will form, then water will drop into the chocolate and it will be ruined.

Chocolate can also be melted in the microwave oven; follow manufacturer's instructions.

CHOCOLATE CURLS

Melt cooking chocolate (either dark or Melts), spread a thin layer over a cool surface such as ceramic tile, granite or marble, allow to set at room temperature. Then, carefully holding a large, sharp knife at about a 45° angle, pull the knife gently over the chocolate to form curls of varying sizes and shapes.

CHOCOLATE SHAVINGS

Use a vegetable peeler to shave mini curls from a block of chocolate.

CHOCOLATE LACE

Melt cooking chocolate (either dark or Melts), pipe onto baking paper, waxed paper or foil in lacy pattern. Allow to set at room temperature for best results.

CHOCOLATE FLAKES

Spread plastic food wrap tightly onto an upturned oven tray or similar flat surface; smooth out any creases or wrinkles. Melt cooking chocolate or Melts, spread a thin layer over the plastic wrap. Allow to set at room temperature, gently lift plastic and break chocolate into flakes.

HOW TO TOAST COCONUT

Place desired amount of desiccated, flaked or shredded coconut in a small heavy-based frying pan. Stir over medium heat until coconut is light golden brown. Turn immediately onto a heatproof tray to cool before using. Leftover cold toasted coconut will keep indefinitely in an airtight container in the refrigerator.

HOW TO TOAST ALMONDS

Toast almonds on an oven tray in a moderate oven about 7 minutes or until lightly browned; cool before using.

ORANGE SHREDS

1. You can make orange shreds several hours ahead; keep, covered, at room temperature. Using a vegetable peeler, peel rind thinly from oranges. Cut rind into thin strips. Place ½ cup (110g) sugar in a small saucepan, add ¼ cup (60ml) water, stir over heat, without boiling, until sugar is dissolved. Add rind, simmer 5 minutes.

2. Remove rind from syrup to tray to cool before using. Any type of citrus peel can be done this way.

FEATHER AND FAN

1. This simple but effective decoration is made by piping lines of icing or melted chocolate (with a few drops of oil added) on the surface of icing or cream. It is important that both the surface and the piped chocolate are soft while making the pattern.

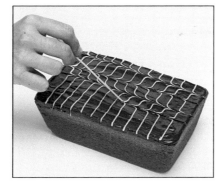

2. Carefully pull a skewer through the lines of icing in 1 direction, then in the opposite direction, as shown.

HOW TO MAKE A PAPER PIPING BAG

Use greaseproof paper or baking paper. Cut paper into triangles, twist into a cone shape, fold over the top, as shown, or secure with sticky tape. Place icing, chocolate or cream, etc., in bag, gently ease icing down into bag, fold over top, cut hole in tip of bag with scissors to required size.

HOW TO LINE CAKE PANS

As a guide, when baking cakes which take longer than 1 hour to cook, there should be a 5cm "collar" of paper above the edge of the pan to protect the top of the cake. The following method of lining round or square cake pans allows for this. Use greaseproof or baking paper.

1. For side/s, cut 3 paper strips long enough to fit around the pan, and 8cm wider than the depth of the pan. Fold strips lengthways about 2cm from edge and make diagonal cuts about 2cm apart up to the fold, as pictured. This enables the paper to fit readily around the curves or corners of the pan, with cut section fitting around the base.

2. Using base of pan as a guide, cut 3 paper circles to cover base of pan; place paper base in position.

123

Glossary

Here are some terms, names and alternatives to help everyone

understand and use our recipes perfectly.

ALLSPICE: pimento in ground form.

ALMONDS:

Flaked: sliced nuts.

Ground: we used packaged commercially ground nuts.

Slivered: nuts cut lengthways.

ARROWROOT: used mostly for thickening. Cornflour can be used instead.

BACON-FLAVOURED CHIPS: also known as crisps.

BAKING PAPER: also known as parchment paper.

BAKING POWDER: is a raising agent. It is mostly made from cream of tartar and bicarbonate of soda in the proportions of 1 level teaspoon cream of tartar to ½ level teaspoon bicarbonate of soda. This is equivalent to 2 level teaspoons baking powder.

BICARBONATE OF SODA: baking soda.

BUTTER: use salted or unsalted (also called sweet) butter; 125g is equal to 1 stick butter.

CHEESE:

Cottage: fresh, white, unripened curd cheese; we used a low-fat variety.

Cream: also known as Philly.

Parmesan: sharp-tasting hard cheese used as a flavour accent. We prefer to use fresh parmesan cheese, although it is available already finely grated.

Tasty: matured cheddar; use a hard, good-tasting variety.

CHERRIES:

Glace: are cooked in heavy sugar syrup and then dried.

Maraschino: are preserved in sugar syrup with flavourings and colour; sometimes have stems.

CHOCOLATE: we used good-quality compounded cooking chocolate.

Choc Bits (morsels): are buds of dark chocolate; they do not melt in cooking.

Milk Melts: are discs of milk chocolate ideal for melting and moulding.

COCOA: cocoa powder.

COCONUT: use desiccated coconut unless otherwise specified.

Essence: extract.

Flaked: flaked and dried coconut flesh.

Milk: available in cans.

Shredded: thin strips of dried coconut.

COFFEE AND CHICORY ESSENCE: a slightly bitter syrup based on sugar, caramel, coffee and chicory. If not available, dissolve 2 teaspoons instant coffee powder and 1 tablespoon brown sugar in 1 tablespoon boiling water.

COLOURINGS: we used concentrated liquid food colourings.

CORNFLOUR: cornstarch.

CREAM: light pouring cream, also known as half and half.

Sour: a thick commercially cultured soured cream.

Thickened (whipping): double cream or cream with more than 35 percent fat can be substituted.

CUSTARD POWDER: vanilla flavoured pudding mix.

ESSENCE: extract.

FLOUR:

Rice: flour made from rice; ground rice can be substituted.

Soya: creamy-coloured flour processed from soya beans.

White plain: unbleached all-purpose flour.

White self-raising: substitute plain (unbleached all-purpose) flour and baking powder in the proportions of 1 cup (150g) plain flour to 2 level teaspoons baking powder. Sift together several times before using.

Wholemeal plain: whole-wheat all-purpose flour.

Wholemeal self-raising: whole-wheat self-raising flour; add baking powder to all-purpose flour as above to make wholemeal self-raising flour.

GOLDEN SYRUP: maple, pancake syrup or honey can be substituted.

GRAND MARNIER: an orange-flavoured liqueur.

GROUND RICE: rice flour can be substituted.

HAZELNUTS, GROUND: we used packaged commercially ground nuts.

HAZELNUT SPREAD: Nutella.

JAMS AND CONSERVES: preserves of sugar and fruit.

JELLY CRYSTALS: fruit-flavoured gelatine crystals.

KUMARA: orange sweet potato.

LAMINGTON PAN: 20cm x 30cm rectangular pan, 3cm deep.

LEMON-FLAVOURED SPREAD: available in jars from supermarkets.

MALT EXTRACT: barley sprouted, dried, crushed and evaporated to a thick, syrupy consistency.

MILK: we used full-cream homogenised milk unless otherwise specified.

Buttermilk: is now made by adding a culture to skim milk; skim milk can be substituted.

Evaporated: unsweetened canned milk from which water has been extracted.

Full-cream milk powder: concentrated milk solids; when reconstituted with water has a similar content to fresh milk.

Sweetened condensed: we used milk which has had 60 percent of the water removed, then sweetened with sugar.

MIXED DRIED FRUIT: a combination of sultanas, raisins, currants, mixed peel and cherries.

MIXED PEEL: a mixture of crystallised citrus peel; also known as candied peel.

MIXED SPICE: a blend of ground spices usually consisting of cinnamon, allspice (pimento) and nutmeg.

MOLASSES: the end product of raw sugar manufacturing or refining.

OIL: polyunsaturated vegetable oil.

RIND: zest.

RUM: we use an underproof rum (not overproof) for a more subtle flavour.

SEMOLINA: a hard part of the wheat which is sifted out and used mainly for making pasta.

SUGAR: we used coarse granulated table sugar, also known as crystal sugar, unless otherwise specified.

Brown: a soft, fine, granulated sugar containing molasses.

Castor: also known as superfine; is fine granulated table sugar.

Icing: also known as confectioners' sugar or powdered sugar. We used icing sugar mixture.

Raw: natural brown granulated sugar.

SULTANAS: golden raisins.

TOASTED MUESLI: toasted granola.

TREACLE: golden syrup or honey can be substituted.

UNPROCESSED BRAN: outer layer of most cereal grains.

WHEATGERM: small creamy-coloured flakes milled from the embryo of wheat.

Index

QUICK CONVERSION GUIDE

Wherever you live in the world, you can use our recipes with the help of our easy-to-follow conversions for all your cooking needs. These conversions are approximate only. The difference between the exact and approximate conversions of liquid and dry measures amounts to only a teaspoon or two, and will not make any noticeable difference to your cooking results.

MEASURING EQUIPMENT

The difference between measuring cups internationally is minimal within 2 or 3 teaspoons' difference. (For the record, 1 Australian metric measuring cup will hold approximately 250ml.) The most accurate way of measuring dry ingredients is to weigh them. When measuring liquids use a clear glass or plastic jug with metric markings.
If you would like metric measuring cups and spoons as used in our Test Kitchen, turn to page 128 for details and order coupon. In this book we use metric measuring cups and spoons approved by Standards Australia.
● a graduated set of 4 cups for measuring dry ingredients; the sizes are marked on the cups.
● a graduated set of 4 spoons for measuring dry and liquid ingredients; the amounts are marked on the spoons.
● 1 TEASPOON: 5ml
● 1 TABLESPOON: 20ml

**NOTE: NZ, CANADA, USA AND UK ALL USE 15ml TABLESPOONS.
ALL CUP AND SPOON MEASUREMENTS ARE LEVEL.**

DRY MEASURES

METRIC	IMPERIAL
15g	½oz
30g	1oz
60g	2oz
90g	3oz
125g	4oz (¼lb)
155g	5oz
185g	6oz
220g	7oz
250g	8oz (½lb)
280g	9oz
315g	10oz
345g	11oz
375g	12oz (¾lb)
410g	13oz
440g	14oz
470g	15oz
500g	16oz (1lb)
750g	24oz (1½lb)
1kg	32oz (2lb)

LIQUID MEASURES

METRIC	IMPERIAL
30ml	1 fluid oz
60ml	2 fluid oz
100ml	3 fluid oz
125ml	4 fluid oz
150ml	5 fluid oz (¼ pint/1 gill)
190ml	6 fluid oz
250ml	8 fluid oz
300ml	10 fluid oz (½ pint)
500ml	16 fluid oz
600ml	20 fluid oz (1 pint)
1000ml (1 litre)	1¾ pints

**WE USE LARGE EGGS
WITH AN AVERAGE
WEIGHT OF 60g**

HELPFUL MEASURES

METRIC	IMPERIAL
3mm	⅛in
6mm	¼in
1cm	½in
2cm	¾in
2.5cm	1in
5cm	2in
6cm	2½in
8cm	3in
10cm	4in
13cm	5in
15cm	6in
18cm	7in
20cm	8in
23cm	9in
25cm	10in
28cm	11in
30cm	12in (1ft)

HOW TO MEASURE

When using the graduated metric measuring cups, it is important to shake the dry ingredients loosely into the required cup. Do not tap the cup on the bench, or pack the ingredients into the cup unless otherwise directed. Level top of cup with knife. When using graduated metric measuring spoons, level top of spoon with knife. When measuring liquids in the jug, place jug on flat surface, check for accuracy at eye level.

OVEN TEMPERATURES

These oven temperatures are only a guide; we've given you the lower degree of heat. Always check the manufacturer's manual.

	C˚ (Celsius)	F˚ (Fahrenheit)	Gas Mark
Very slow	120	250	1
Slow	150	300	2
Moderately slow	160	325	3
Moderate	180	350	4
Moderately hot	190	375	5
Hot	200	400	6
Very hot	230	450	7

TWO GREAT OFFERS FROM THE AWW HOME LIBRARY

Here's the perfect way to keep your Home Library books in order, clean and within easy reach. More than a dozen books fit into this smart silver grey vinyl folder. PRICE: Australia $9.95; elsewhere $19.95; prices include postage and handling. To order your holder, see the details below.

All recipes in the AWW Home Library are created using Australia's unique system of metric cups and spoons. While it is relatively easy for overseas readers to make any minor conversions required, it is easier still to own this durable set of Australian cups and spoons (photographed). PRICE : Australia: $5.95; New Zealand: $A8.00; elsewhere: $A9.95; prices include postage & handling.
This offer is available in all countries.

TO ORDER YOUR METRIC MEASURING SET OR BOOK HOLDER:

PHONE: Have your credit card details ready. **Sydney:** (02) 260 0035; **elsewhere in Australia:** 008 252 515 (free call, Mon-Fri, 9am-5pm) or *FAX* your order to (02) 267 4363 or *MAIL* your order by photocopying or cutting out and completing the coupon below.

PAYMENT: **Australian residents:** We accept the credit cards listed, money orders and cheques. **Overseas residents:** We accept the credit cards listed, drafts in $A drawn on an Australian bank, also English, New Zealand and U.S. cheques in the currency of the country of issue.
Credit card charges are at the exchange rate current at the time of payment.

Please photocopy and complete coupon and fax or send to:
AWW Home Library Reader Offer, ACP Direct, PO Box 7036, Sydney 2001.

❑ Metric Measuring Set   ❑ Holder
Please indicate number(s) required.

Mr/Mrs/Ms _____

Address _____

_____

Postcode_____ Country _____

Ph: (   ) _____ Bus. Hour:_____

I enclose my cheque/money order for $ _____ payable to ACP Direct

OR: please charge my:

❑ Bankcard ❑ Visa ❑ MasterCard ❑ Diners Club ❑ Amex

☐☐☐☐☐☐☐☐☐☐☐☐☐☐☐☐☐ Exp. Date ___/__

Cardholder's signature_____

(Please allow up to 30 days for delivery within Australia. Allow up to 6 weeks for overseas deliveries.)

Both offers expire 31/12/93.   AWRB92